JOYS OF HAWAIIAN COOKING

Favorite Recipes of Big Island Cooks

JOYS OF HAWAIIAN COOKING

Favorite Recipes of Big Island Cooks

edited by
Martin and Judy Beeman

illustrated by
Mark Waters

Published by the
PETROGLYPH PRESS, LTD.
160 Kamehameha Avenue
Hilo, Hawai'i 96720
Telephone (808) 935-6006
Toll Free (888) 666-8644
Fax (808) 935-1553
PetroglyphPress@hawaiiantel.net
www.BasicallyBooks.com

Printed by Hilo Bay Printers

Copyright 1977
by Pikake Publishers

ISBN# 912180-41-2

First Edition
First Printing, 1977
Second Printing, 1979

Second Edition
Eleven Printings, 1981-2003
Twelfth Printing
July, 2007

TABLE OF CONTENTS

PAU HANA TIME

* CLAM DIP *

1 (3 oz.) pkg. cream cheese   ½ tsp. Tabasco sauce
1 can minced clams, reserve juice

Beat cream cheese until soft, add clams amd some clam juice slowly until the right thickness is achieved. Then add the Tabasco sauce.

— — —

* DIP FOR RAW VEGETABLES *

1 cup sour cream, imitation   4 tsps. curry powder
   will do   4 drops Tabasco sauce
1 cup mayonnaise   2 tsps. dry grated onion

Mix all ingredients together. Refrigerate 2 hours. Use as a dip for celery, carrot sticks, mushrooms, cucumbers and cauliflower.

— — —

* AVOCADO CLAM DIP *

2 large ripe avocados (2 cups,diced) lemon juice
1 cup light cream   salt to taste
½ cup minced clams with liquid   cayenne pepper
½ cup chilled chicken broth   minced chives

Cut avocados in half and remove skin and seed. Dice the fruit. Beat smooth with a rotary beater and then slowly add the cream. Blend in clams and chicken broth. Beat until smooth. Season with a drop or two of lemon juice, salt and a dash of cayenne pepper. Pile into a large serving bowl. Sprinkle surface with chopped chives. Serve with unsalted crackers, biscuits or melba toast. Makes 3½ cups of dip.

— — —

* CRAB DIP *

1 can crab meat   1 garlic bud, chopped or mashed
1 (3 oz.) pkg. cream cheese   (or garlic powder)
½ cup mayonnaise   dash of salt and pepper
½ can condensed tomato soup   MSG
                                     6 - 8 drops Tabasco sauce

Soften the cream cheese, add the mayonnaise and tomato soup. Then add the garlic, salt, pepper, MSG and Tabasco. Mix well, then add the crab. Doubling all ingredients except crab will still produce a good "crabby" dip.

CALIFORNIA CHEESE TOPPING FOR FRENCH BREAD OR ROLLS

3 green onions, chopped fine
½ lb. cheddar cheese, grated
1 (8 oz.) pkg. cream cheese
1 cup mayonnaise

1 tsp. Salad Supreme
1 tsp. mustard
dash of Worcestershire
salt and pepper

After the cream cheese has softened, combine all the ingredients together until thoroughly mixed. Spread mixture on French bread or rolls. Sprinkle the top with additional Salad Supreme. Broil until the cheese melts. Cut into bite-size pieces as a party pupu.

— — —

* MINI CHICKEN LEGS *   350° oven

½ lb. chicken wings (about 8)
milk

4 tbsps. dry seasoning mix
   (B-B-Q or teriyaki)

Break off the wing tips at the joints, and discard, leaving mini chicken legs. Dip in milk and roll in seasoning. Bake in a 350° oven for about 45 minutes or until done.

— — —

* GUACAMOLE DIP I *

2 medium avocados, mashed
2 tsps. lemon juice
grated onion to taste
1 tomato, chopped fine

Tabasco
1 cup grated cheddar cheese
enough mayonnaise to moisten

Mix all ingredients in a bowl. Serve with taco chips, corn chips, or vegetable sticks.

— — —

* GUACAMOLE DIP II *

5 - 6 large avocados
   (4 cups chopped)
1 (3 oz.) pkg. cream cheese
⅓ cup green pepper, finely chopped
½ cup jalapeno pepper, finely
   chopped

1 tsp. Worcestershire sauce
¼ tsp. Tabasco sauce
salt and pepper to taste
2 hard-boiled eggs, finely chopped

Cut avocados in half, remove seeds and skins. Chop and combine with cream cheese. Mash until smooth. Add the next 5 ingredients. Pile into a bowl and sprinkle with hard-cooked eggs. Serve as a dip with crackers or as a salad.

— — —

* BARBECUED MEAT STICKS *

2 lbs. thinly sliced beef
½ cup soy sauce
5 tbsps. brown sugar
½ clove garlic, minced

¼ tsp. ginger powder
1 tbsp. oil
3 doz. bamboo skewers

Slice beef into one-inch strips, about six inches long. Blend the rest of the ingredients. Marinate the meat in the sauce for at least 20 minutes. Skewer meat on bamboo sticks. Broil over charcoal or in oven broiler.

— — —

* LOMI LOMI SALMON *

½ lb. smoked salmon
4 tomatoes, cut in half
4 large green peppers, chopped

3 scallions, chopped
1 onion, chopped
1 cup crushed ice

Scoop out pulp from the tomatoes, reserving shells. Shred the salmon and combine all ingredients except ice. Fold in crushed ice and serve cold in the tomato halves.

— — —

* SHERRIED TUNA DIP *

2 (3 oz.) pkgs. cream cheese
1 tbsp. mayonnaise
5 tbsps. sherry
1 (6 oz.) can grated tuna
2 tbsps. capers, optional

2 tbsps. parsley, chopped
½ tsp. Worcestershire sauce
1 tsp. salt
1 tsp. grated onion

Mash cream cheese with a fork. Blend in mayonnaise and gradually add sherry, beating until smooth. Add remaining ingredients and mix well. Heap in a serving bowl and serve accompanied by crackers or potato chips.

— — —

* RUMAKI *   450° oven

12 slices bacon
½ lb. chicken livers (about 6)
12 water chestnuts
3 tbsps. soy sauce

2 tsps. sugar
¼ tsp. MSG
pinch of ground ginger
toothpicks

Cut bacon strips in half and fry until partially cooked but still soft. Cut chicken livers into quarters. Slice the water chestnuts in half. Combine the rest of the ingredients and add to livers. Marinate for 20 minutes. Wrap chicken livers and water chestnuts in the bacon strips and skewer in place with the toothpicks. Place on a rack in 450° oven for ten minutes. Put in fresh toothpicks before serving.

— — —

* MARINATED EEL *

2 lbs. cleaned eel
3 cloves garlic
all purpose flour, for coating
olive oil for frying

¼ tsp. oregano
salt
¼ fresh chili, chopped
1½ cups red wine vinegar

Rinse eel and dry. Cut into two-inch pieces. Peel one clove of garlic and cut in half. Rub the eel with cut sides of garlic and coat with flour. Peel and slice remaining garlic. Heat oil until very hot, add eel and saute until brown. Drain well and place in a non-metal bowl in layers alternating with layers of the seasonings. Pour the wine vinegar into a saucepan and reduce to one-third over high heat. Remove pan from heat, mix in three tbsps. of the frying oil and pour over eel. Set aside and marinate for at least 24 hours, preferably two to three days. Serve cold as a pupu.

— — —

* HAM AND CHIPS *

1 pkg. cream cheese
1 small can deviled ham
¼ tsp. dry mustard
¼ tsp. pepper

1 tbsp. minced onion
dash of Worcestershire sauce
dash of Tabasco sauce
salt to taste

Mix all of the above ingredients. Cream to a thin consistency. Pile into a bowl and serve with assorted chips.

— — —

* MEATBALL PUPUS *

1 lb. ground beef
salt and pepper

5 ozs. beer
½ cup catsup

Season meat with salt and pepper. Form into small meat balls. Place in skillet, cover with catsup and beer and cook over high heat, about five minutes. Shake pan now and then to prevent burning. Serve in sauce.

— — —

* VIENNA SAUSAGE PUPUS *

4 cans Vienna sausage
¾ cup brown sugar
½ cup white sugar
½ tsp. MSG
Worcestershire sauce

1 tsp. dry mustard
1 tbsp. catsup
⅔ cup soy sauce
⅓ cup water

Cut sausages in half. Mix together the rest of the ingredients. Fry sausages in the sauce. Take sausages out of the pan while the syrup is still runny. Serve warm.

— — —

* CRISP WONTON *

1 cup ground pork	1 egg, beaten
½ cup chopped water chestnuts	½ tsp. MSG
3 tbsps. scallions, chopped	1 pkg. wonton wrappers
2 tsps. soy sauce	2 cups oil

Combine first six ingredients. Place one-half tsp. filling on the diagonal of a wonton wrapper. Fold on diagonal. Moisten opposite edges together to seal in the filling. Bring the two opposite corners of the diagonal toward the center, moisten and press together to seal. Deep fry wontons until golden brown. Drain and serve hot.

— — —

* CHA-GIO *
(Vietnamese Spring Rolls)

2 lbs. ground pork (pork hash)	1 tsp. MSG
1 can crab meat	½ tsp. each salt and pepper
½ lb. frozen shrimp, finely chopped	2 pkgs. spring roll shells
¾ pkg. dried mushrooms, soak in water to soften, then chop fine	5 eggs, beaten
	1 onion, chopped fine
1 pkg. (2 oz.) long rice, soak until soft, then cut into 1-inch pieces	

Mix together all of the above ingredients except the spring roll shells. Pat the shells with water to make them pliable. Tear the shells in half and then put a tbsp. of filling in each half. Fold the shell around the filling. Fry in a pan of hot oil, about one-inch deep, with folded side do down. Turn and fry until light brown. Continue process until all filling is used.

— — —

* TAHITIAN RAW FISH *

1 lb. fresh raw fish	2 tbsps. chopped scallions
1 tsp. coarse salt	1 clove garlic
juice of 6 limes	1 cup coconut milk

Cut fish into bite size pieces. Sprinkle with salt and cover with lime juice. Cover and refrigerate at least four hours. Drain off the lime juice. Add the rest of the ingredients. Chill until time to serve. Arrange on a bed of lettuce.

— — —

* CRAB AND SHRIMP CANAPES *   375 ° oven

1 (8 oz.) pkg. cream cheese	6 - 8 oz. shelled cooked shrimp
½ cup mayonnaise	6 - 8 oz. water chestnuts, optional
4 tbsps. minced green onion	1 (6 oz.) can crab
1 tsp. lemon juice	2 pkgs. refrigerated butterflake
⅔ cup grated cheddar cheese	dinner rolls
salt to taste	Parmesan cheese
MSG	

Beat cream cheese until smooth. Add mayonnaise, onions, lemon juice, grated cheese, salt and MSG. Blend. Put shrimp and water chestnuts through a food grinder. Add to cream cheese mix. Flake crab and add to the cheese mixture. Separate each butterflake roll into separate sections. Cut each section in two, flatten and put a spoonful of mixture in each and cup the dough up around the filling. Put a pinch of Parmesan cheese on top of each. Bake on an ungreased baking sheet for 12 to 15 minutes in a 375 ° oven. Serve warm.

— — —

* EGGPLANT CHIPS *   200 ° oven

1 medium eggplant	1 large clove garlic, crushed
salt	cooking oil
1½ cups cornmeal	

Slice eggplant into one-eighth inch thick slices. With a salt shaker, salt lightly each slice and stack slices into two stacks. Weight each pile with a saucer to force out the excess liquid. Let stand for one hour. Dip each slice in cornmeal. Place garlic in a large skillet with one-half inch oil and heat. When oil is hot, fry a few slices at a time until golden brown, turning once. Do.not overlap slices. In between batches, add more oil if necessary. Drain on paper towels and place in baking dish. Bake in a 200 ° oven until all chips are done. Do not cover baking dish. Serve hot.

— — —

* KOREAN MEATBALLS *

3 lbs. ground beef	2 tbsps. scallions, chopped
¼ cup soy sauce	½ clove garlic, minced
1 tbsp. oil	15 whole water chestnuts, sliced
1 tsp. sesame seed oil, optional	3 eggs, beaten
4 tsps. sugar	flour to dredge
½ tsp. MSG	

Mix together the first eight ingredients. Roll into three-fourths inch balls. Place each meat ball on a slice of water chestnut. Coat with flour, then dip into beaten eggs. Fry in hot, well-greased skillet. Turn over and cook until done. Drain on paper towels. Serve hot. To reheat, place in

continued

a 300 oven for five minutes.
Variation: Water chestnuts may be chopped and added to the meat.
Continue as above.

— — —

* CHEESE WAFERS *   375 ° oven

¼ lb. butter or margarine, softened 1 cup flour
½ lb. extra sharp cheddar cheese   ½ tsp. paprika

Grate the cheese and mix well with the butter. Add flour and form into balls, about the size of a large marble. Sprinkle with paprika. Bake in a 375 ° oven for seven to ten minutes on an ungreased cookie sheet. These freeze well. Makes about 60 wafers.

— — —

* CHEESE BALLS *

2 (8 oz. pkgs.) cream cheese,   dash of Tabasco
  softened   ¼ cup chopped nuts
1 (5 oz.) jar blue cheese spread   ¼ cup minced parsley
1 (5 oz.) jar cheese spread   ¼ cup sesame seeds, toasted
1 tsp. minced onion   2 tbsps. poppy seeds
2 tsps. Worcestershire sauce

Combine and beat cheese, spreads, onion and sauces until smooth. Refrigerate for several hours or overnight, until firm. Roll into small bite-size balls, then roll each ball in a mixture of nuts, parsley and seeds. Chill or freeze until ready to use. Makes about 100 balls.

— — —

* CHEESE CUBES *   375 ° oven

Cut fresh bread into cubes of any size. Beat one egg with one and one-fourth tbsps. melted butter.   Dip cubes into egg mixture and roll in finely grated cheese, seasoned with a little salt and cayenne pepper. Bake cubes on a greased baking sheet in a 375 ° oven until the cheese melts. Serve hot on toothpicks.

— — —

* STUFFED MUSHROOM CAPS *

1 lb. fresh mushrooms   salt and pepper to taste
½ cup bread crumbs   ¼ cup melted butter
¼ tsp. thyme   2 tbsps. parsley
¼ tsp. oregano   4 tbsps. sherry

Mix thoroughly the bread crumbs, thyme, oregano, salt, pepper, parsley and sherry. Wash the mushrooms and remove the stems. Chop the stems and saute in the butter for 10 minutes. Cool and then mix with the sherry spice mixture. Fill caps with the mixture and place on a baking sheet. Broil until hot. Serve with toothpicks.

— — —

* KAHLUA *

2 cups instant coffee
8 cups sugar
4 cups boiling water

1 fifth rum, brandy or vodka
1 vanilla bean, slashed

Mix together the coffee, sugar and boiling water. Let this mixture cool and then add the rum and vanilla bean. Store in a glass gallon bottle or jar. Shake occasionally. Don't open for at least four weeks. The longer it sets, the better it gets.

— — —

* BANANA MILK SHAKE *

⅓ cup banana puree
¾ cup fresh or evaporated milk
¼ tsp. vanilla

few grains of salt
1 tsp. sugar
1 egg

Add all ingredients and mix well with an electric beater. Serve icy cold.

— — —

* SPICED TEA *

Boil the juice of two lemons and two oranges with two cups of sugar and one pint of water. Remove from fire. Add one-third cup tea and two-thirds tbsp. cloves tied in cheesecloth. Cover and let steep for one hour. Strain into a pot and set aside until ready to use. Add hot water to dilute to taste. Heat and serve.

— — —

* FRESH GUAVA FRUIT PUNCH *

½ finger of fresh ginger root
1½ cups water
¾ cup sugar
3 cups medium strength tea

6 ripe guavas
¾ cup orange juice
¼ cup lemon juice
½ cup pineapple juice

Peel and chop the ginger root. Boil ginger with one-half cup of the water until a strong ginger flavor is obtained. Cool and strain through a cloth, squeezing the ginger. Wash guavas, cut and press the pulp through a fine sieve to remove the seeds. Combine all other ingredients and mix well. Serve over ice.

— — —

SOUPS AND SALADS

* CHILLED AVOCADO CREAM SOUP *

1 large ripe avocado
1½ cups chicken broth
1½ tbsps. fresh lime juice
1 tsp. salt

¼ tsp. pepper
½ tsp. chili pepper water or dash
   of Tabasco
½ cup whipping cream

Peel, stone and dice the avocado. Put all ingredients except cream into a blender in order given and blend until smooth. Check seasoning. Add more to taste. Chill covered, and before serving stir in cream.

— — —

* APPLE SOUP *

6 large apples, green and tart	1½ tbsps. arrowroot
2 cups water	1 vanilla bean, sliced lengthwise and
2 cups apple juice	opened, or 2 cinnamon sticks
½ cup honey, or to taste	¼ tsp. nutmeg
juice of one lemon	

Peel and core apples. Add to boiling water and juice. Let steep until apples are soft, about 15 to 20 minutes. Put through a sieve. Put apples into serving bowl and juice into saucepan. Add honey and bring to a boil. While stirring, add arrowroot, dissolved in lemon juice. Add split vanilla bean and let simmer for 2 to 3 minutes while stirring constantly. Add to the apples in the serving bowl and add a dash of nutmeg. Optional: add a spoonful of yogurt before serving.

— — —

* FRENCH ONION SOUP *

5 cups thinly sliced Maui onions	2 qts. beef bouillon
3 tbsps. vegetable oil	½ tsp. basil
3 tbsps. flour	3 - 6 slices toasted French bread
1 cup bourbon	½ cup grated Swiss cheese

In a three quart flame proof casserole, saute sliced onions in vegetable oil until soft. Stir in flour to form paste. Add bourbon, stir until smooth. Gradually stir in bouillon. Season with basil. Simmer 30 to 40 minutes. Top with toasted bread, sprinkle with cheese and broil until cheese is golden and bubbly. Serve immediately.

— — —

* ABALONE SOUP *

3 chicken bouillon cubes	4 water chestnuts, sliced
4 cups water	4 dried mushrooms, soaked in one
giblets from one chicken	cup of water for ½ hour
¼ inch thick slice of fresh ginger	2 stalks of Chinese cabbage, cut into
½ tsp. salt	one inch pieces
juice from one can of abalone	¾ cup canned abalone, sliced
½ tsp. MSG	

Combine the first four ingredients and simmer for one and one-half hours. Strain. Add the abalone juice and season with the salt and MSG. Add water chestnuts to stock. Discard water and stems of mushrooms and slice. Add mushrooms to soup. Cook for three minutes. Add cabbage and cook for another minute. Serve garnished with abalone slices. Do not cook abalone in soup because it will become tough.

— — —

* WONTON SOUP *

1 pkg. wonton wrappers	1 small egg
½ lb. ground pork and/or shrimp	½ tsp. MSG
⅔ cup water chestnuts, chopped	¼ tsp. salt
1 tbsp. soy sauce	2 quarts chicken broth
⅓ cup scallions, chopped	

Combine pork, water chestnuts, scallions, soy sauce and egg. Mix well, then sprinkle with MSG and salt. Place a rounded teaspoon of filling in the diagonal of a wonton square. Fold over so that a filled triangle is formed. Wet the edges to seal. Press together. Bring chicken stock to a boil. Season to taste. Drop wontons in boiling stock and cook covered for five minutes or until wontons rise to the surface. Serve hot.

— — —

* THANKSGIVING SALAD *

1 (6 oz.) pkg. strawberry Jello	1 (12 oz.) carton small curd cottage
1 (10 oz.) can crushed pineapple,	cheese
drained	1 cup chopped nuts
4½ oz. Cool Whip or whipped	1 (8 oz.) jar maraschino cherries
cream	1 cup fresh strawberries, optional
2 oz. shredded coconut	

Follow directions for Jello on back of package and chill. Just before Jello completely thickens, add crushed pineapple, Cool Whip, shredded coconut, cottage cheese and nuts. Mix well. Chop cherries into small pieces and add, leaving four cherries whole for decoration. Pour salad into mold and let set. For a more colorful salad, add some of the juice of the cherries.

— — —

* AVOCADOS *

For neat slices, peel the avocado first, then slice lengthwise on the seed and remove in slices. For neat halves, cut avocados in half first, and twist to loosen flesh from seed. Remove seed, then peel.

— — —

* FRUIT-FILLED AVOCADOS *

Cut avocados in half lengthwise. Scoop out flesh with a ball cutter. Combine avocados with cubed pineapple, cut orange and grapefruit sections and halved seedless grapes. Sprinkle fruits with lemon juice and a little powdered sugar. Fill avocado shells, and serve on a bed of lettuce. Serve with salad dressing of your choice.

— — —

* AVOCADO AND COTTAGE CHEESE SALAD *

3 avocados
1 tbsp. lemon juice
¾ tsp. salt
2 cups cottage cheese

1½ tsps. minced onion, or 2 tsps.
   minced chives
1 tbsp. minced parsley
dash of paprika

Cut avocados in half and put one tsp. of lemon juice in each and season with salt. Fill avocados with cottage cheese that has been mixed with the onion or the chives and the parsley.

— — —

* AVOCADO COCKTAIL *

4½ cups diced avocados
½ tsp. salt
1 cup catsup

1 tsp. finely chopped onion
1½ tbsps. lemon juice
½ tsp. Worcestershire sauce

Sprinkle salt over the avocados and chill. Combine the other ingredients, chill, and pour over the diced avocados just before serving. Serve in cocktail glasses as a first course.

— — —

* LYCHEE CHICKEN SALAD *

2 lbs. chicken breasts
1½ cups water
1 large onion, chopped
1 sm. piece of ginger root, crushed
1 tsp. salt
1½ tsps. curry powder

2 (11 oz.) cans mandarin oranges
1 (1 lb. 4 oz.) can lychees or fresh
   lychees, deseeded
⅔ cup mayonnaise
1 tbsp. lemon juice
½ tsp. grated orange rind

Debone the chicken. In a saucepan combine chicken, water, onion, ginger, salt and one-half tsp. of the curry powder. Cover and bring to a boil. Lower heat and simmer for 20 minutes or until chicken is cooked. Cool chicken in stock. Use stock for soup. Cut chicken in chunks. Drain the mandarin oranges and lychees, reserving one tbsp. of the lychee syrup. Combine chicken, mandarin oranges and lychees and chill. Combine mayonnaise, lemon juice and orange rind. Stir in the lychee syrup and the remaining one tsp. curry powder. Pour over salad and mix lightly. Serve on lettuce leaves.

— — —

* FAIRY SALAD *

1 pkg. lime Jello
1 pkg. lemon Jello
2 cups hot water
1 (8¼ oz.) can crushed pineapple
¾ cup mayonnaise

1 carton cottage cheese
½ cup chopped walnuts
Maraschino cherries, chopped
2 pkgs. Dream Whip, prepared as
   as directed on package

continued

Dissolve Jellos in hot water. When Jello starts to set, take from refrigerator and add remaining ingredients in order given. Makes one large bowl.

— — —

* AVOCADO SURPRISE *

1 pkg. lime Jello	2 tbsps. lemon juice
1 cup boiling water	2 tsps. chopped onion
½ cup sour cream	½ tsp. celery salt
½ cup mayonnaise	½ cup green pepper, chopped
1 cup pecans, chopped	12 whole pecans for garnish
1 avocado, mashed	

Dissolve Jello in boiling water and refrigerate until slightly thickened. Whip until foamy, then fold in sour cream and mayonnaise. Add chopped pecans, avocado, lemon juice, onion, celery salt and pepper. Place pecan halves in bottom of a one quart Jello mold, then pour Jello mixture on top and refrigerate until firm.

— — —

* PINEAPPLE CRAB SALAD *

2½ cups diced fresh pineapple	1½ tbsps. catsup
1½ cups shredded crab meat	1 tsp. Worcestershire sauce
⅔ cup mayonnaise	

Mix pineapple and crab together and arrange on lettuce leaves. Mix the rest of the ingredients and pour over salad.

— — —

* AVOCADO STUFFED ARTICHOKES *

6 large artichokes	½ tsp. sugar
1 tbsp. salt	2 medium avocados
4 tbsps. vinegar	2 tsps. lemon juice
8 qts. boiling water	¾ cup mayonnaise
4 tbsps. wine vinegar	12 (2 oz.) anchovy fillets, chopped
6 tbsps. salad oil	and drained
3 tbsps. olive oil	1 tbsp. capers, drained
1 tsp. salt	½ tsp. salt
¼ tsp. pepper	¼ tsp. crushed red pepper
½ tsp. dry mustard	

Cut the stems off the artichokes, leaving flat bottoms. Remove the tough outside leaves. Add salt, vinegar and artichokes to boiling water. Cook 30 - 40 minutes or until leaves pull out easily and bottoms are tender. Place upside down on a rack to drain thoroughly. When cool, separate the middle leaves and remove the thistle. Combine vinegar, oils, salt, pepper, mustard and sugar. Blend and spoon over artichokes in a non-metal bowl. Cover and refrigerate until chilled. Cut avocados in
continued

half lengthwise, remove seeds and skins. Mash the meat with a fork until smooth. Combine lemon juice, mayonnaise, anchovy fillets, capers, salt and pepper. Drain artichokes. Spoon avocado mixture into centers and serve.

— — —

* CUCUMBER SALAT *
(Danish)

2 - 3 cucumbers	¾ cup vinegar
1 tbsp. salt	1 tbsp. honey, to taste
¼ tsp. black pepper	1 tbsp. parsley or dill

Score cucumbers with the tines of a fork. Slice thin and place in a bowl. Sprinkle salt over cucumbers and let sit for 1 to 2 hours. Drain well. Mix the rest of the ingredients and pour over cucumbers.

— — —

* BANANA WALDORF SALAD *

1½ cups diced ripe bananas	⅓ cup chopped nuts
1½ cups diced apples	¾ cup mayonnaise
1 cup diced celery	

Chill ingredients before dicing, then dice and combine with nuts and mayonnaise. Serve on lettuce leaves and sprinkle with lemon juice. Serve immediately.

— — —

* CHEESE MOLD *

1 pkg. lime Jello	1 cup crushed pineapple
1½ cups hot water	½ cup chopped celery
1 cup cottage cheese	½ cup chopped nuts

Combine the Jello and hot water and chill until partially set. Mix the rest of the ingredients together and stir into Jello. Pour into an oiled mold. Chill until firm. Unmold on lettuce leaves and garnish with mayonnaise. Sprinkle with paprika.

— — —

* BAKED PAPAYA *   350° oven

1 large firm ripe papaya	¾ tsp. salt
1 tbsp. butter	2 tbsps. lemon juice

Pare and cut papaya lengthwise into six pieces. Remove the seeds. Sprinkle with salt, lemon juice and butter. Place in a baking pan, add enough water to cover bottom of pan to prevent burning and bake in a 350° oven for 35 minutes. Serve immediately. Serve in place of a vegetable.

— — —

* MELON BALLS IN PORT *

Fill sherbert glasses with balls of watermelon, honeydew and cantaloupe. Pour two tbsps. port wine over each glass of fruit. Chill well before serving.

— — —

* BAKED STUFFED AVOCADO *   350° oven

3 avocados
¼ cup lime juice
2 cups flaked crabmeat, tuna or chicken
1 cup canned cream sauce

dash of salt and pepper
dash of cayenne
2 tbsps. green pepper, diced
1 tsp. minced onion
1 cup grated cheddar cheese

Cut avocados in half lengthwise. Remove seeds. Sprinkle avocado meat with lime juice and salt. Combine crabmeat, tuna or chicken with cream sauce. Season to taste with all ingredients except cheese. Fill avocados and sprinkle with cheese. Arrange avocados in baking pan with one-half inch of water in the bottom. Bake in a 350° oven for 15 minutes until cheese melts and avocado is heated through.

— — —

* CABBAGE PINEAPPLE SALAD *

¼ lb. (2 cups) head cabbage, shredded
½ cup celery
⅔ cup fresh pineapple, diced

2 tbsps. mayonnaise, or French dressing
⅛ tsp. salt
1 tbsp. fresh pineapple juice

Mix all ingredients together. Serve cold. A good dish to serve with barbecued fish.

— — —

* FRUIT SALAD *

1½ boxes orange Jello
1 pint cottage cheese, small curd
1 can crushed pineapple

1 can mandarin oranges
1 pint Cool Whip
1 cup shredded coconut

Mix all ingredients together. Refrigerate several hours before serving.

— — —

* POTATO SALAD *

5 lbs. potatoes	8 hard-boiled eggs, diced
1 medium onion, finely chopped	2 tbsps. white vinegar
dill pickles to taste, chopped	2 tbsps. mustard
6 tbsps. lemon juice	1 cup mayonnaise

Boil potatoes until tender. Run cold water over potatoes when done to prevent them from cooking more. Drain. Peel if desired and dice into small pieces. Pour lemon juice and vinegar over the potatoes. Then add the rest of the ingredients and mix well. Refrigerate until cold and ready to serve.

— — —

* BAKED GRAPEFRUIT *   400° oven

1 large grapefruit	2 tbsps. honey
2 tbsps. cognac or fine brandy	1 tbsp. brown sugar

Cut grapefruit in half. Remove seeds. Separate pulp from pith all around grapefruit. Loosen pulp from dividing membrane. Sprinkle each half with half of the rest of the ingredients. Place in a baking dish containing about one-fourth inch of water. Bake in a 400° oven for about 15 to 20 minutes. Serve hot.

— — —

* BLUE CHEESE SOUR CREAM DRESSING *

1 cup sour cream	dash of white pepper
1 tbsp. white wine vinegar	½ tsp. dry mustard
1 tbsp. fresh lemon juice	¼ cup (2 oz.) blue cheese, crumbled
½ tsp. salt.	
Optional to add:	
1 tbsp. finely chopped onion	1 tbsp. olive oil

Blend all of the ingredients and refrigerate.

— — —

* FRENCH DRESSING *

1 cup salad oil	½ tsp. Worcestershire sauce
1 medium bottle of catsup	dash of salt, pepper, paprika and
3 tbsps. sugar	garlic salt
¾ cup vinegar	

Combine all ingredients and mix well.

— — —

* ITALIAN SALAD DRESSING *

Base: 4 tsps. salt
1 tsp. dried minced garlic
1 tsp. black pepper

4 tsps. instant minced onions
1 tsp. sugar
1 tsp. paprika

Combine all of the above. This is the base for the salad dressing. To make the salad dressing, add one and one-half tsps. of the above mixture to the following:
2 tbsps. water   ⅔ cup oil
¼ cup vinegar

Mix well and serve over vegetable salads.

— — —

* TANGY TOMATO DRESSING *

1 can tomato soup
1 tsp. salt
⅓ cup honey
1 tsp. paprika
2 tsps. mustard
¼ cup lemon juice

2 tbsps. vinegar
1 tbsp. chopped onion
1 clove garlic
2 tsps. Worcestershire sauce
¾ cup salad oil

Place all ingredients except salad oil in blender. When smooth gradually add salad oil.

— — —

* HONEY DRESSING FOR FRUIT SALAD *

⅓ cup sugar
1 tsp. dry mustard
1 tsp. paprika
1 tsp. celery seed
¼ tsp. salt

⅓ cup honey
5 tbsps. vinegar
1 tbsp. lemon juice
1 tsp. onion juice
1 cup salad oil

Mix well and pour over fruit salad.

— — —

* FRUIT SALAD DRESSING *

2 egg yolks, beaten
juice of one lemon

½ tsp. salt
2 tbsps. powdered sugar

Mix well and pour over fruit salad.

— — —

* AVOCADO GRAPEFRUIT DRESSING *

½ cup mashed avocado   ½ cup grapefuit juice
½ tsp. salt

Press avocado through a coarse sieve. Add the other ingredients and mix well until a smooth paste is obtained. Chill and serve with a vegetable salad.

— — —

* FRUIT JUICE FRENCH DRESSING *

1 tbsp. sugar or honey   dash of pepper
½ tsp. paprika   2 tbsps. lemon juice
¼ tsp. dry mustard   ¼ cup grapefruit juice
¾ tsp. salt   1 cup salad oil

Combine all ingredients in a jar and shake well.

— — —

* PASSION FRUIT DRESSING *

½ cup passion fruit juice   2 tbsps. sugar
½ cup salad oil   ½ tsp. celery seed
1 tsp. salt   1 clove garlic
1 tsp. paprika

Place all ingredients in a blender. Cover and blend for one minute. If passion fruit nectar is used, omit the sugar. Serve over fruit salads.

— — —

SEAFOOD

HAWAIIAN FISH LIST

Aku.	ocean bonito
A'awa.	sandfish
Ahi.	tuna
Ahipalah.	albacore
Awa.	milkfish
Ahaaha.	needlefish
A'u.	swordfish
Akule.	mackerel
Amaama.	mullet
He'e.	squid
Hapuupuu.	black sea bass
Humuhumunukunukuapuaa.	triggerfish
Kawakawa.	bonito
Kaku.	barracuda
Kalikali.	small snapper
Kumu.	goatfish
Kahala.	amberfish
Malolo.	flying fish
Mahimahi.	dolphin
Manini.	surgeonfish
Manono.	goatfish
Moi.	threadfin
Ono.	giant mackerel
Opakapaka.	large snapper
Opelu.	mackerel
Oio.	bonefish
Opihi.	shellfish
Papio.	young ulua
Pualu.	surgeonfish
Puhi.	eel
Poopaa.	rock cod
Ukihikihi.	Moorish idol
Ula.	snapper
Ulaula.	goatfish
Ulua.	giant pompano
Uu.	squirrelfish
Weke.	goatfish

* AKU AND AHI *

Aku and ahi are tender and cook quickly, so do not overcook these fish. For best eating, saute in a skillet with a small amount of oil or margarine, or, broil with a little barbecue sauce. Sashimi is a popular island favorite served at almost every get-together, fancy or informal. Ahi is the most favored fish for this dish.

— — —

* SAUTEED AKU OR AHI *

1 lb. fillet of fish	2 tbsps. flour
salt and pepper	2 tbsps. oil

Cut fillet into three-fourth inch slices. Salt, pepper and lightly coat with flour. Saute in skillet with a small amount of oil. When the fish is done squeeze lemon or lime juice over all the pieces and serve with soy sauce. Serve immediately.

— — —

* BROILED AKU OR AHI *

1 lb. fresh fillet of fish	1 piece ginger root, crushed
¼ cup soy sauce	¼ tsp. MSG
1 tbsp. sugar	2 tsps. salad oil

Slice the fillet. Mix together the rest of the ingredients and soak the fish in this sauce. Broil and serve immediately.

— — —

* AKUBURGER OR AHIBURGER *

1 lb. fillet of fish	2 stalks green onion, chopped
1 egg	2 tbsps. flour
1½ tsps. salt	2 tbsps. oil
¼ lb. onion, chopped	

Chop or grind up the fish until fine. Add egg to flour and beat until smooth. Add the remaining ingredients excluding the oil. Heat the oil in a skillet and drop the mixture by tbsps. full into the skillet. Fry until brown and cooked through. Serve with soy sauce.

— — —

* SASHIMI *

1 lb. fillet of fresh ahi (never frozen)

Remove any skin or dark flesh from the ahi. Cut fillet into rectangles, one inch thick and two inches wide. With a sharp knife, slice fish diagonally into one-eighth inch slices. Arrange attractively on a serving dish. Make a sauce out of the following:

* SAUCE *

½ tsp. dry mustard   ½ cup soy sauce
½ tsp. hot water

Make a paste with the mustard and hot water, stirring with a chopstick as the water is added. Add soy sauce and mix well. Dip the raw fish into sauce as it is eaten.

— — —

* FISH LOAF *   350° oven

1 tbsp. lemon juice   ½ cup bread crumbs
2 cups canned fish, flaked   1 tbsp. chopped parsley
¼ cup oil   1 tsp. minced onion
½ cup flour   ¾ tsp. salt
1 cup milk   tomato sauce
½ cup chopped celery

Add lemon juice to fish. Melt oil, stir in flour, then add milk and cook until mixture is smooth and thick. Allow to cool. Then add fish flakes, celery, bread crumbs, parsley and salt and mix until well blended. Mold into a loaf shape with your hands, and place on an oiled paper in an open roasting pan. Bake in a 350° oven for 45 minutes. Serve with tomato sauce if desired.

— — —

* LUAU FISH BAKE *   350° oven

1 (4 - 5 lbs.) whole fish   Hickory smoke flavored BBQ sauce
2 cups stuffing prepared from   salt
   package mix   butter
½ cup celery, sauteed   pineapple slices
½ cup green pepper, sauteed

Prepare stuffing according to package directions, add celery and green pepper. Stuff the fish. Tie soft string around the fish, closing the opening. Place fish on heavy foil and brush generously with barbecue sauce. Sprinkle with salt and dot with butter. Seal the foil around the fish. Place fish on a shallow pan and bake 1 hour in a 350° oven. Remove from oven and turn back foil, brush with additional barbecue sauce and bake 15 minutes longer or until the fish can be flaked with a fork. Garnish with pineapple slices.

— — —

* BARBECUED FISH *   375° oven

1 (4 - 5 lbs.) fish	2 drops Tabasco sauce
2 tbsps. salad oil	2 tbsps. Worcestershire sauce
2 tbsps. vinegar	1 tsp. salt
½ cup catsup	¼ tsp. pepper
¼ cup water	¼ tsp. dry mustard
½ cup chopped onion	½ tsp. chili powder
1 clove garlic, minced	1 (6 oz.) can mushrooms

Place cleaned fish in foil. Combine the rest of the ingredients in a saucepan and heat. Pour sauce over fish and bake in a 375° oven for 25 to 30 minutes.

— — —

* STEAMED FISH WITH BLACK BEAN SAUCE *

3 tbsps. black beans	1½ tbsp. oyster sauce
⅛ tsp. MSG	1 bunch green onions
1 large clove garlic, minced	1 chunk pickled turnip
1 small chunk ginger, peeled and sliced	2 tbsps. Scotch Whiskey
⅛ tsp. peanut oil	2 whole fresh fish (1½ lbs. each)

Wash the black beans and then crush with a spoon. Sprinkle MSG over black beans. Mix the rest of the ingredients except the fish. Add no salt as there is enough salt in the rest of the ingredients. Clean the fish and put two tbsps. of the sauce in each cavity. Pour the rest of the sauce over the fish. Steam for about 10 minutes.

— — —

* FRIED ONO OR MAHIMAHI *

1 lb. fish	1 cup crushed round crackers
salt and pepper	oil for frying
2 beaten eggs	

Slice fish into one-half inch thick pieces. Season with salt and pepper. Dip fish into beaten egg and then roll in crushed crackers. Fry in oil until browned.

— — —

* FISH FILLETS BAKED IN WINE AND MUSHROOM SOUP *

3 tbsps. butter or margarine	2 tbsps. grated Parmesan cheese
3 tbsps. flour	2 tbsps. chopped parsley
1 cup cream of mushroom soup	1 lb. fish fillets
½ cup white wine	

continued

Melt the butter in a saucepan and stir in flour. Add soup and wine and cook, stirring constantly until the mixture boils and thickens. Add cheese and parsley and arrange fillets in a single layer in a greased shallow baking dish or in three or four individual casseroles. Pour sauce over fish. Bake in a 375° oven for 25 minutes or until fish is tender.

— — —

* AKU PORTUGUESE STYLE *

1 lb. fresh aku
1 sliced onion
1 tsp. pepper sauce

1 clove garlic, crushed
vinegar
3 tbsps. oil

Dice the aku into bite-size cubes. Place in a bowl and add onion, salt, pepper, garlic, and cover everything with vinegar. Let stand for 4 hours or more. Saute the fish in oil and serve immediately.

— — —

* CRAB LORRAINE *　　　　350° oven

9-inch pastry pie crust
7 oz. can drained crabmeat
½ lb. shredded or diced Swiss
　cheese
1½ cups light cream
½ tsp. salt

¼ tsp. nutmeg
dash of pepper
½ cup diced ham
4 eggs
1 thin slice onion

Prepare pie crust. Sprinkle crabmeat and cheese on bottom of crust. Put remaining ingredients into blender and blend for 6 to 10 seconds. Pour mixture into pie crust. Bake in a pre-heated oven for 60 minutes at 350° or until top is golden brown and mixture is set. Serve warm.

— — —

* AHI STEAMED WITH LEMON *

2 ahi fillets
salt, pepper and flour
3 or 4 garlic buds, grated
oil for frying

3 large onions, sliced
¼ - ½ cup butter
MSG
2 lemons, sliced

Score the fillets with a knife and rub in the salt, pepper and garlic. Fry in oil until light brown on both sides, then sift flour to cover the fish on both sides. Place fish on the side of the pan and saute the onions. Season with salt and pepper. Slice the butter and place on fish. Add water for gravy and MSG. Put onions over fish. Cover pan and steam over low heat, basting occasionally. When the fish is white and firm, serve and enjoy. Garnish with lemon slices.

— — —

* FISH WITH COCONUT *

fish (as much needed)   ti leaves
salt   coconut milk

Salt the fish. Fill cavity with coconut milk and tie up in ti leaves. Broil on coals over a barbecue pit.

— — —

* SALMON MOUSSE *   350° oven

1¾ lbs. thin salmon steaks   3 egg whites
1 pint heavy cream   salt
1 cup mayonnaise   white pepper
1 tsp. minced onion   Hollandaise sauce (see sauces)
2 tbsps. lemon juice   parsley for garnish
¼ tsp. celery salt

Preheat oven to 350° and put in a pan of water large enough to accommodate the mold or molds to be used. Butter the mold or molds. Remove all skin and bones from the fish, and then dice. Combine the cream, mayonnaise, onion, lemon juice and celery salt in a mixing bowl. Pour approximately one-third of this mixture into a blender. Add one-third of the salmon and one egg white. Blend at medium high speed until smooth. Put the mousse into a bowl and repeat this process until the egg whites and the rest of the ingredients are gone. Salt and pepper to taste. Fill the mold or molds with the mixture and cover with buttered aluminum foil. Place in the pan of hot water and bake for 45 minutes for the large mold and 25 minutes for the small ones. They should be firm on top. Remove from the oven and let stand for 5 minutes. Unmold and cover with Hollandaise sauce. Garnish with parsley. Serve as a main dish or as a first course for dinner.

— — —

* SALMON LOAF *   350° oven

1 lb. canned salmon   ½ cup chopped sweet pickles
¾ cup soft bread crumbs   1 tsp. salt
¾ cup milk   2 tsps. melted butter
1 beaten egg

Mix all of the above ingredients together and pack into a greased loaf pan. Bake in a 350° oven for 45 minutes.

— — —

* SALMON STEAKS WITH AVOCADO BUTTER *

6 - 8 salmon steaks, one inch thick

Marinade:
½ cup peanut oil
½ cup olive oil
4 tbsps. lemon juice
1 clove garlic, sliced
1 small onion, sliced
½ cup chopped parsley
1 tbsp. Worcestershire sauce
1 tbsp. soy sauce
½ tsp. black pepper

Avocado Butter:
1 large ripe avocado
¼ lb. soft butter
1 small clove garlic, pressed
2 tsps. lemon juice
1 tbsp. Worcestershire sauce
salt and pepper

Place salmon steaks in a shallow, ceramic dish. Combine the ingredients for the marinade and spoon over the steaks. Marinate at least 4 hours in the refrigerator, turning the steaks occasionally. Drain the steaks 15 minutes before cooking. Make the avocado butter by peeling the avocados and mashing the meat with the rest of the ingredients. Broil the steaks over charcoal, 5 minutes on each side. Or broil in the oven. Serve steaks with avocado butter. Serve immediately.

— — —

* JELLIED FISH SALAD *

2 tbsps. gelatin
½ cup cold water
2 eggs
¾ tsp. salt
¼ cup minced celery

1 tsp. minced onion
¼ cup vinegar
¼ cup water
2 cups cooked fish flakes
mayonnaise

Soften the gelatin in cold water. Beat the eggs. Add the salt, celery, onion, vinegar and water. Cook over boiling water until thick. Add the softened gelatin and stir until it has dissolved. Then add the fish. Pour into dampened molds. Let stand in the refrigerator until set. Turn out on crisp lettuce leaves and serve with mayonnaise.

— — —

* SEAFOOD SALAD *

1 can tuna, salmon or crab
1 can shrimp
2 tbsps. French dressing
1 cup diced celery
½ cup sliced cucumber
2 tbsps. chopped radish

2 tbsps. lemon or lime juice
salt, pepper, paprika
lettuce, sliced thin
2 green onions, chopped
½ cup mayonnaise

Flake the tuna into a bowl. Devein the shrimp. Add the French dressing to the tuna and shrimp and let stand for 15 minutes. Add the vegetables and seasonings and mix lightly. Place the mixture on a bed of greens and serve immediately. Garnish with lemon slices and extra slices of cucumber. Serve the mayonnaise separately.

— — —

* CLAM CAKES *

1 can minced clams with liquid   pancake mix

Mix enough pancake mix with clams and juice to make a batter. Add water or skim milk if liquid in the can is slight. A beaten egg may be added if desired. Cook as you would for pancakes.

— — —

* SEAFOOD MEDLEY *

½ lbs. scallops
1 tsp. salt
1 cup water
½ pint oysters
1 cup cooked shrimp
3 tbsps. butter
1 cup mushrooms
1½ tbsps. finely chopped green
   onion

3 tbsps. flour
½ cup thin cream
2 tsps. sherry
2 tsps. lemon juice
1 cup bread crumbs
1 tbsp. melted butter
½ cup grated cheese
dash of paprika

Cut the scallops into small cubes, add one-half tsp. salt and the water and simmer for 15 minutes. Drain, reserving stock. Drain oysters, reserving liquid. Combine scallop stock, oyster liquid and shrimp stock to make 1 cup liquid. If more liquid is needed for the cup, add milk. Heat butter, add mushrooms and onion. Cook over low heat for about 5 minutes. Blend in flour and slowly add seafood liquid. Cook until thickened, stirring constantly. Add cream, sherry, lemon juice, remaining salt and seafood. Place the mixture into a baking dish. Sprinkle with a crumbled mixture of bread crumbs, melted butter and cheese. Sprinkle with paprika. Broil for a few minutes until mixture is browned and bubbly.

— — —

* CRAB CAKES *

1 lb. cooked crab meat
3 slices bread, soaked in milk and
  squeezed
1 tsp. prepared mustard
1 tsp. chopped parsley

1 tsp. Worcestershire sauce
2 slightly beaten eggs
salt and pepper
½ cup oil

Combine crab, softened bread, mustard, parsley, Worcestershire and eggs. Mix well and season to taste with salt and pepper. Shape into about eight patties. Fry in hot oil on each side until golden brown. Serve hot.

– – –

* SALMON CROQUETTES *

1 egg, beaten
2 tbsps. green onion
salt and pepper

½ can salmon, undrained
1 tsp. lemon juice
6 - 8 crackers, crushed

Mix all of the above ingredients and shape into patties. Fry lightly in a non-stick pan or in a small amount of oil.

– – –

* BATTER FRIED FISH *

2 lbs. white fish
1 cup flour
2 tbsps. baking powder
1 tsp. salt

1 egg, separated
½ cup lukewarm water
1 tbsp. melted shortening
hot oil for frying

Cut up the fish into serving pieces. Sift flour, baking powder, and salt into a bowl. Drop the egg yolk into the center. Add the water and the melted shortening. Mix well. Fold in the beaten egg white. Dry the fish pieces and dip in batter. Fry in deep hot oil for 4 to 6 minutes or until golden brown.

– – –

* BAKED AVOCADO WITH SEAFOOD *

2 avocados, halved
juice of one lemon
3 tbsps. water
¾ cup mayonnaise
½ tsp. curry powder

1½ cups crabmeat, shrimp or lobster
1 tbsp. capers
2 hardboiled eggs, quartered
½ cup buttered crumbs

Brush avocado halves with the lemon juice. Blend together water, mayonnaise and the remaining lemon juice. Simmer over low heat. Stir in curry powder. Add seafood, capers and eggs. Mix well. Fill avocados with seafood mixture and top with buttered crumbs. Broil for 3 to 4 minutes until crumbs are browned. Serve hot.

– – –

* FRIED PRAWNS WITH HOT MUSTARD SAUCE *

1 beaten egg	1 cup flour
1 cup ice water	2 tbsps. melted butter
½ tsp. sugar	1 lb. fresh prawns
½ tsp. salt	

Mix together all of the above ingredients except the prawns. Beat until smooth. Remove the shells and veins from the prawns. Wash and dry the prawns carefully, then dip in batter and fry to a goldem brown in deep fat. Serve hot with catsup or hot mustard or both.

* HOT MUSTARD *

Stir 6 tbsps. boiling water into 3 tbsps. dry mustard. Add 2 tsps. oil and ½ tsp. salt.

— — —

* SHRIMP PUFF *   325 ° oven

6 slices very fresh white bread	3 slightly beaten eggs
¾ cup cooked shrimp	2 cups milk
¾ cup grated cheese	½ tsp. salt
dry mustard	¼ tsp. paprika
dash of cayenne	

Trim the crusts from the very fresh bread. Spread lightly with butter, then cut into small squares. Spread half of the bread squares in the bottom of a greased casserole. Add a layer of shrimp and cheese. Season with a dusting of dry mustard and cayenne. Repeat layers. Combine the eggs and milk. Season with the salt and paprika. Pour over the bread-shrimp mixture. Bake in a 325 ° oven for 40 minutes.

— — —

* SHRIMP AND MUSHROOMS *

2 cans sliced celery	2 tbsps. cold water
2 cans sliced mushrooms, drain and reserve liquid	1 tsp. instant beef bouillon
	1 cup water
1 tbsp. soy sauce	2 cans (4½ oz.) shrimp rinsed and
1 tsp. ground ginger	drained
2 tbsps. cornstarch	2 - 3 cups hot cooked rice

Cook and stir celery, mushroom liquid, soy sauce and ginger in a large skillet until celery is crisp-tender, about 5 minutes. Mix cornstarch and water until smooth. Stir cornstarch mixture, bouillon and water into celery mixture. Cook, stirring constantly until mixture thickens and boils. Boil and stir for 1 minute. Stir shrimp and mushrooms into the mixture. Heat through, stirring constantly. Serve over rice.

— — —

* ISLAND SHRIMP CURRY *

6 tbsps. butter
2 tsps. minced ginger
1 onion, finely chopped
6 tbsps. flour
1½ tsps. salt
2 - 3 tbsps. curry powder

1 cup milk
2 cups coconut milk
2 lbs. fresh shrimp, shelled and
   cleaned
½ tsp. MSG

Melt the butter. Add minced ginger and chopped onions and cook until onions are soft. Add flour, salt, curry powder and stir until blended. Add milk. Mix until sauce thickens. Add coconut milk and shrimp and cook over low heat for 15 minutes. Stir occasionally. Season with MSG. Serve over hot rice with condiments.

— — —

* SHRIMP MOLOKAI *

2 lbs. raw shrimp
1 cup pineapple juice
1 cup sherry
3 tbsps. lemon juice
1 clove garlic, crushed

6 peppercorns
1 whole bay leaf
hot pepper sauce to taste
1 stick (¼ lb.) butter
sesame seeds

Shell and devein the shrimp. Place in a bowl, together with a mixture of all the ingredients except the butter and sesame seeds. Marinate for 2 to 3 hours. Strain shrimp and brush with the melted butter. Roll shrimp in the sesame seeds and cook lightly in a buttered pan until they turn pink. Boil the remaining marinade liquid for 10 minutes to reduce it, then strain and use as a dip for the shrimp.

— — —

* PANNED OYSTERS *

1 qt. good-sized oysters
2½ tbsps. butter
⅓ tsp. salt

⅛ tsp. white pepper
1 tbsp. sherry
3 tbsps. apple brandy

Wash the oysters. Melt the butter in a chafing dish. Add the salt, pepper, sherry, brandy and then the oysters. Cook gently until the edges curl. Serve on buttered toast.

— — —

* TUNA CORN CHOWDER *

2 cans tuna
1 can condensed cream of potato
   soup
3 cups milk
1 tbsp. butter

1 tbsp. grated onion
1 small bay leaf
dash of pepper
1 (8 oz.) can whole kernel corn

Drain tuna and break up into large pieces. Combine soup, milk, butter, onion, bay leaf and pepper. Heat until hot. Add corn and tuna and heat through again. Remove bay leaf. Garnish with parsley.

— — —

* FRIED ABALONE *

Although abalone as purchased in fish markets is well pounded, it doesn't do any harm to give it a few extra taps with a wooden mallet before cooking. To fry, dip one-fourth inch thick slices in lightly seasoned beaten egg. Roll in fine dry cracker crumbs and fry in hot butter in a heavy skillet. Allow not more than 2 minutes to each side. Serve hot with a wedge of lemon.

— — —

* CHINESE TUNA *   350° oven

1 can tuna
1 can Chinese noodles
1 can mushroom soup
¾ cup water
1 cup diced celery

1 cup sliced onions
1 cup sliced pepper
1 can mushroom pieces
1 cup cashew nuts, chopped

Mix all ingredients together in a casserole. Let stand for 1 hour and then bake in a 350° oven for 30 minutes.

— — —

* TUNA PUFFS *   325° oven

4 tbsps. butter or margarine
½ lb. sliced mushrooms
4 tbsps. flour
1 tsp. salt
few grains cayenne
1½ cups milk

4 eggs, separated
hot sauce
1 cup grated cheese
1 (7 oz.) can tuna
2 cups fresh bread crumbs

Melt butter in skillet, add mushrooms and cook for 5 minutes. Remove mushrooms, add flour and blend well. Add seasonings and milk, cook, stirring constantly, until thickened. Beat egg yolks slightly, add a small amount of hot sauce and blend. Add yolks to sauce and cook 2 minutes. Fold in grated cheese. Remove from heat. Add drained, flaked tuna and bread crumbs, and cool. Beat egg whites until stiff and fold into fish
continued

mixture. Pour into six large buttered custard cups or individual casseroles. Bake at 325 ° for 45 minutes or until firm. Serve with lemon wedges. If a large casserole is used, bake for 1¼ hours.

— — —

* TUNA CASSEROLE *
350 ° oven

1 pkg. spinach noodles
2 cans chunky tuna

1 lb. sharp cheddar cheese, grated
Parmesan cheese, grated

Boil the spinach noodles in water to cover until tender. Meanwhile, in a large baking dish or casserole, mix the undrained tuna and the cheddar cheese. When noodles are done, drain and add to the tuna cheese mixture. Mix well. Top with Parmesan cheese and bake in a 350 ° oven until hot and bubbly, about 35 to 40 minutes, depending on the depth of the pan. This recipe makes the best tuna casserole in the world. This is only true if no substitutions are used for the ingredients.

— — —

* TUNA BROCCOLI LOAF *
375 ° oven

5 eggs
½ cup milk
1 cup soft bread crumbs
2 cans tuna, drained
1 tbsp. grated onion
1 tsp. lemon juice

½ tsp. salt
⅛ tsp. pepper
dash of nutmeg
½ cup grated Swiss cheese
1 pkg. frozen chopped broccoli,
    cooked and drained

Beat eggs, milk and bread crumbs together in a large bowl. Let stand for 15 minutes. Stir in tuna, onion, lemon juice, salt, pepper, nutmeg and Swiss cheese. Place cooked broccoli into the blender, cover and blend until smooth. Stir into tuna mixture. Turn into a greased 4x8 inch loaf pan. Bake in a 375 ° oven for 1 hour. Let stand 5 minutes before turning out onto a serving dish.

— — —

POULTRY

* TERIYAKI CHICKEN *

6 whole chicken breasts, boned
1 tbsp. ginger
⅓ cup soy sauce

2 tbsps. sugar
3 tbsps. dry sherry or sake
½ tsp. MSG

Remove bones from chicken. Flatten meat with mallet or slice into one-fourth inch thick fillets. Combine the rest of the ingredients. Marinate the chicken in this sauce for 20 minutes. Broil meat over charcoal or in broiler.

— — —

* EASY LEMON CHICKEN *   400° oven

Sauce:
1 tbsp. soy sauce
½ tsp. salt
½ tsp. pepper
¼ cup salad oil
½ cup lemon juice
2 tbsps. grated lemon peel
1 large clove garlic, crushed

Chicken:
½ cup flour
1 tsp. salt
¼ tsp. pepper
2 tsps. paprika
3½ lbs. fryer, cut in pieces
½ cup butter, melted

Combine all sauce ingredients. Refrigerate at least 1 hour. In a heavy paper bag, combine flour, salt, pepper and paprika. Shake a few chicken pieces at a time in the bag to coat them. Put chicken, skin side down, in single layer in shallow baking pan. Brush with all the butter. Bake uncovered, for 30 minutes at 400°. Turn chicken and pour the sauce over the chicken. Bake 30 minutes or longer until the chicken is golden brown. Serve with rice to take advantage of the delicious sauce.

— — —

* BARBECUED CHICKEN *

5 lbs. chicken thighs, preferably
    frozen
2 inch finger ginger root, sliced

1½ cup shoyu
⅔ cup sugar
2 oz. sweet white wine

In a large bowl, mix ginger, shoyu, sugar and wine. Marinate chicken while it is defrosting for 4 hours or more. Stir occasionally to separate chicken as it defrosts. Broil chicken over hot coals, turning frequently.

— — —

* ORANGE CHUTNEY CHICKEN *   350° oven

3 lbs. chicken breasts, thawed
1 tsp. salt
¼ tsp. pepper
2 tbsps. salad oil
½ cup orange juice
½ cup chutney, chopped

¼ cup sugar
2 tbsps. lemon juice
2 oranges, peeled and cut into ½
    inch slices
1 tbsp. cornstarch
2 tbsps. water

Sprinkle chicken with salt and pepper. Heat oil and brown chicken. Place chicken in a 13x9x2 inch baking pan. Pour orange juice over chicken, cover and bake in a 350° oven for 45 minutes. Combine chutney, sugar, and lemon juice. Place orange slices over chicken and pour the sauce over all. Continue baking uncovered for 15 minutes, until chicken is tender. Remove chicken to a serving platter. Combine cornstarch and water. Place baking pan with the sauce on stove top and bring the liquid to a boil. Lower heat and stir in the cornstarch mix. Pour sauce over chicken and serve.

— — —

* SESAME CHICKEN WINGS *

3 lbs. chicken wings
2 eggs
2 stalks green onions, sliced
2 cloves garlic, grated
1 small piece ginger, grated
½ tsp. MSG
1 tbsp. toasted sesame seeds

1 tbsp. sherry
4 tbsps. flour
8 tbsps. cornstarch
4 tbsps. sugar
1½ tbsps. salt
5 tbsps. soy sauce

Cut the wing tips off the chicken. Combine all the rest of the ingredients and mix. Marinate the wings overnight. Deep fry until golden brown. Serve as main dish or pupu.

— — —

* BAKED CHICKEN IN SOUR CREAM *   375° oven

1 egg
3 tbsps. water
1 roasting chicken, cut up
¾ cups sifted flour

1 cup bread crumbs
6 tbsps. butter
salt and pepper
2 cups sour cream

Beat egg slightly and add cold water. Dip the chicken pieces in flour, then egg and water, and then bread crumbs. Brown in butter. Remove to baking pan, sprinkle with salt and pepper and set in a 375° oven. Heat sour cream to liquify. After 1 hour of baking, pour a little hot sour cream over each piece. Repeat in 15 minutes, finishing all the sour cream. Total baking time is 1½ hours. The chicken will absorb all the cream. To make gravy, remove chicken and add 2 tbsps. butter in roasting pan. Add 2 tbsps. flour and mix until smooth. Add 2 cups milk. Stir constantly and simmer 3 to 4 minutes. Pour over chicken or serve separately.

— — —

* CHICKEN HEKKA *

2 lbs. chicken thighs
1 bunch green onions
1 bunch watercress
shoyu

sugar
2 onions, sliced
1 block tofu
1 bundle Japanese long rice

Cut chicken in long thin strips, cut onions and watercress in 1 inch long lengths. Brown the chicken in a little fat, and add shoyu and sugar to taste. Simmer. Add onions, tofu and long rice. Cook until the chicken is tender. Add watercress just before serving. Optional: Bamboo shoots sliced very thin and Japanese dry mushrooms soaked in water until soft and sliced in thin strips leaving a few whole for garnish.

— — —

* CHICKEN AND ALMONDS *
(good for leftovers)

2 tbsps. butter
1 tbsp. minced onion
¼ cup flour
¾ cup milk
¾ cup chicken broth
½ cup white wine

1 tsp. sugar
2½ cups diced chicken, cooked
½ cup split, toasted almonds
2 egg yolks
½ cup cream
salt and pepper to taste

Melt the butter in a skillet. Add onion and brown slightly. Blend flour with milk and pour into a separate saucepan along with the chicken broth, wine and sugar. Cook stirring constantly, until thickened. Add the chicken, onions and almonds. Heat thoroughly. Pour a small amount of the hot mixture into egg yolks and then return yolks to chicken mixture. Add the cream and cook 1 minute, stirring constantly. Add salt and pepper to taste. Serve in pastry shells, over toast or crisp noodles.

— — —

* DEEP FRIED SWEET-SOUR CHICKEN *   375° oven

1 (4 lb.) chicken, cooked
2 tbsps. cornstarch
2 tbsps. soy sauce

1 tsp. salt
2 eggs
oil for frying

Skin and debone chicken. Cut into 1 inch cubes. Combine cornstarch and soy sauce and mix well. Combine salt and eggs in mixer bowl and beat with a whisk or rotary beater until light. Stir in cornstarch mixture until just blended. Heat oil in a deep fat fryer to 375° or until a small ball of flour mixed with water floats to the top immediately. Dip the chicken cubes into the egg mix and drain slightly. Drop in the chicken, several cubes at a time, in oil and fry until lightly browned. Drain on paper towels. Place chicken in individual serving dishes and spoon sweet-sour sauce all over chicken.

— — —

* SWEET-SOUR SAUCE *

¾ cup sugar
2 tbsps. soy sauce
1 tbsp. wine vinegar

3 tbsps. catsup
2 tbsps. cornstarch
½ cup water

Combine the first four ingredients in a saucepan and bring to a boil. Dissolve the cornstarch in the water and add to sauce. Cook over low heat, stirring until sauce thickens. Pour over chicken.

— — —

* CHICKEN MACADAMIA *

3 whole chicken breasts, boned
1 tsp. MSG
salt
2 eggs
½ cup flour
¼ cup cornstarch
½ cup cold water
¼ cup vinegar

⅓ cup water
1 tsp. minced ginger
1 medium onion, grated
¼ tsp. pepper
2 tbsps. oil
2 tbsps. soy sauce
2 tbsps. brandy

Sauce:
2 tbsps. brown sugar
2 tbsps. soy sauce
2 tbsps. cornstarch

1 tbsp. pimento, chopped (or red pepper)
½ cup chopped unsalted macadamia nuts

Sprinkle chicken breasts lightly with salt and MSG. Let stand for 30 minutes. Combine the rest of the ingredients for batter and beat until smooth. Marinate the chicken breasts in the batter for 20 minutes. Fry in deep hot oil. Drain and place in serving platter. Place in a warm oven. Combine all the ingredients for sauce except the pimento and nuts. Simmer for 15 minutes, stirring often. Fold in pimento and pour sauce over chicken. Sprinkle with nuts and serve.

— — —

* CHICKEN BREASTS PIQUANT *   375 ° oven

4 chicken breasts or 1 cut-up
  frying chicken
1½ cups rose or dry red wine
½ cup salad oil
4 tbsps. water

2 cloves garlic, sliced
2 tbsps. ground ginger
½ tsp. oregano
2 tbsps. brown sugar

Arrange chicken in a baking dish. Combine all other ingredients and pour over the top. Bake in a 375 ° oven for 1 hour. Serve over rice.

— — —

* CHICKEN PAPAYA *

2 lbs. chicken thighs
1 medium green papaya
1 medium onion
3 cloves garlic, crushed

4 slices fresh ginger
2 tsps. salt
1 tsp. pepper
2 tsps. MSG

Peel green papaya and cut into 1½ inch slivers, ¼ inch thick. Cut onion in half lengthwise and slice. Debone the chicken and cut each piece into 4. Brown the chicken in hot oil. Place the chicken in a large saucepan and add papaya slivers. Cook over medium high heat, stirring frequently until the papaya is tender. Add seasonings and the onion. Stir well.

Thicken mixture if desired with ¼ cup cornstarch and ½ cup water. Stir in after adding the onions. Cover pot and remove from heat. Let stand a few minutes and then serve hot with rice.

— — —

* CHICKEN CURRY WITH SEEDLESS GRAPES * 325° oven

8 - 10 chicken breasts
¼ lb. butter
4 tbsps. flour
2 cups chicken broth

1 tbsp. curry powder
2 (8¼ oz.) cans seedless grapes, drained

Simmer chicken until tender. When done remove the chicken, reserving the broth. When cooled, cut into bite-size pieces. Melt butter in a double boiler and add flour. Stir until mixture thickens, then add the broth slowly. Add curry powder and salt and pepper to taste. Add chicken and grapes. Let sit for a few hours to let the flavors blend. 1 hour before serving, heat in a 325° oven. Serve with rice and condiments. Condiments: bacon bits, chutney, pineapple, shredded coconut, raisins, chopped nuts, bananas and chopped eggs.

— — —

* CHEESE CHICKEN * 350° oven

½ cup grated Parmesan cheese
¼ cup flour
1 tsp. paprika
½ tsp. salt
dash of pepper

1 (2½ - 3 lb.) chicken, cut-up
1 egg, slightly beaten
1 tbsps. milk
¼ cup margarine, melted

Combine cheese, flour and seasonings. Dip chicken in combined egg and milk and coat with cheese mixture. Place in an oblong baking dish and pour margarine over chicken. Bake in a 350° oven for 1 hour. Sprinkle additional grated cheese over chicken before serving.

— — —

* HISPANIC CHICKEN *
(in a crock-pot)

1 chicken fryer, cooked and boned
1 (10 oz.) can cream of
    mushroom soup
½ cup tomatoes and chilies

2 tbsps. quick cooking tapioca
6 - 8 tortillas, broken into pieces
1 medium onion, chopped
2 cups grated cheddar cheese

Cut cooked chicken into bite-size pieces. Mix chicken well with soup, tomatoes, chilies and tapioca. (Watch the chilies if you do not want it too hot.) Line the bottom of a slow cooker with tortillas. Add one-third of chicken mixture, sprinkle with onions and cheese. Repeat layers of tortillas, chicken, onions and cheese until all ingredients are used up. Cover and cook on low heat for 6 - 8 hours, or cook on high for 3 hours.

— — —

* MACADAMIA STUFFED CHICKEN BREASTS *

4 large chicken breasts
¼ cup coarsely chopped
   macadamia nuts
2 tbsps. finely chopped celery
1 tsp. finely chopped onion
1 tbsp. soft butter

⅛ tsp. salt
& tsp. pepper
1 whole egg, slightly beaten
¼ cup flour, seasoned with salt
   and pepper
4 tbsps. butter

Bone and skin breasts and flatten with cleaver. Mix nuts, celery, onion, butter, salt and papper. Slice chicken breasts in half. Put one quarter of the mixture on each breast, and roll up, turning in ends to secure filling. Pin with skewers. Dip into egg and then flour. Fry until brown and done in a medium hot skillet.

— — —

* JAPANESE CHICKEN AND MUSHROOMS *

⅓ lb. sliced cooked chicken
½ lb. mushrooms
3 onions
6 tbsps. soy sauce
6 tbsps. sherry or sake

6 eggs
1½ lbs. boiled rice
½ tsp. MSG
1 cup chicken broth

Slice the chicken thin, slice mushrooms into 1½ inch long, slice onions lengthwise. Boil the sherry, MSG, soy sauce and chicken stock. Add chicken, mushrooms and onions. Divide this into 6 portions when it has boiled. Put 1 portion into a frying pan and set on the stove. Beat an egg lightly and add it to the pan. When the egg is half cooked, transfer onto the hot rice and cover immediately. Repeat until each portion is used. Serve immediately.

— — —

* ROYAL PINEAPPLE CHICKEN *   400° oven

1 large box frozen chicken thighs
1 cup flour
1 tbsp. salt
1 tsp. pepper
1 large pineapple

4 tbsps. oil
4 tbsps. butter
1 cup grated coconut
1 small can crushed pineapple,
   drained

Bone the chicken, leaving the skin on. Clean the pineapple, removing skin and core. Cut into spears. Roll each thigh around a pineapple spear. Fasten with a toothpick. Dip into seasoned flour. Chill. Melt the butter and oil together in a skillet and brown the chicken thighs. Transfer to a buttered, shallow baking dish. Pour the can of crushed pineapple over chicken and sprinkle with coconut. Bake in a 400° oven for 15 to 20 minutes.

— — —

* ONO CHICKEN PINEAPPLE *

2 small pkgs. frozen chicken thighs
Dust with:
⅓ cup flour
½ tsp. celery salt
¼ tsp. nutmeg
½ tsp. salt

¼ tsp. garlic salt
¾ cup syrup of canned pineapple
2 tbsps. shoyu
1 medium can of pineapple chunks
oil for frying

Shake together the dry ingredients in a paper bag. Add the chicken, a few pieces at a time. Brown the chicken in oil, then drain the fat. Add the pineapple syrup and shoyu. Cover and simmer until tender. Before serving, add the pineapple chunks. Simmer about ½ hour. Add more juice if necessary. If pineapple juice is used instead of the juice from the pineapple, add 2 tbsps. sugar to every ¾ cup juice.

— — —

* YAKITORI *
(Japanese style chicken)

2 (3 - 4 lb.) fryers
1 bunch scallions
2 doz. bamboo skewers
½ cup soy sauce

2 tsps. grated ginger
¼ cup dry sherry or sake
2 tbsps. sugar
toasted sesame seeds

Bone chicken and cut into 1½ inch pieces. Cut scallions into 1¼ inch lengths. String chicken pieces and scallions on bamboo skewers. Make a marinade of the rest of the ingredients. Pour marinade in a deep, narrow jar or glass. Dip skewers of chicken in marinade just before broiling. Broil over charcoal, basting often. Do not overcook. The chicken should be juicy.

— — —

* LUAU CHICKEN *

2 (3 - 4 lb.) fryers, cut-up
4 tbsps. butter
1½ tbsps. salt
1½ cups water
salt and pepper to taste

½ tsp. MSG
3 lbs fresh spinach
3 cups coconut milk (fresh or
  canned)

Brown the chicken in butter. Add salt and water and simmer until chicken is tender. Remove chicken from broth. Add salt, pepper and MSG to season broth. Wash spinach and break into large pieces. Cook without additional water in covered saucepan over low heat until tender. Add 2 cups of hot, but not boiling coconut milk to the spinach and simmer for 2 minutes. Arrange chicken on the center of a large deep dish. Arrange the spinach in coconut milk around the chicken pieces. Heat the remaining cup of coconut milk with chicken broth and pour over chicken and spinach.

— — —

* CHICKEN LONG RICE *

1.bundle long rice
2 (3 - 4 lb.) fryers
2 slices ginger
1 tbsp. salt

dash of pepper
1 tsp. MSG
3 tbsps. chopped scallions
2 tbsps. soy sauce

Soak long rice in warm water for ½ hour. Place chicken in a pot and cover with water. Add ginger and simmer until chicken is tender. Cool. Remove chicken from bones and cut into pieces. Sprinkle chicken with salt, pepper and MSG. Remove ginger from broth and discard. Cut long rice into 4 inch lengths. Add this, scallions and soy sauce to broth. Simmer for 15 minutes, then add chicken. Heat and serve hot.

— — —

* ONE DISH CHICKEN DINNER *   350° oven

2 fryers (3 lb. ea), cut-up
½ cube butter
1 button garlic
1 pkg. frozen peas

2 cans (1 lb. ea.) tiny whole potatoes
1 can (1 lb.) French style string
   beans
2 cans cream of chicken soup

Flour, salt and pepper chicken pieces. Melt the butter in a skillet and add the garlic. Add the chicken and fry both sides until golden brown. Place chicken in baking pan. Add ½ cup water in skillet with butter and pour over chicken. Sprinkle the uncooked frozen peas over chicken. Drain the potatoes and arrange around chicken. Drain and add the beans. Heat soup and add 1½ cans water. Pour soup over casserole. Cover with foil and bake in a 350° oven for 35 minutes, or until chicken is tender. Add ½ cup more water if there is not enough gravy.

— — —

* CHICKEN LIVERS WITH RICE *

⅔ cup rice
½ lb. chicken livers
1 medium onion, cut into
   thin strips
¼ cup margarine

1 can condensed tomato soup
⅓ cup water
1 tsp. chili powder
¼ tsp. lemon juice

Cook the rice. Meanwhile, cut livers into small pieces. Brown the livers and onion lightly in 2 tbsps. margarine. Stir in soup, water, chili powder and lemon juice. Simmer uncovered for 15 minutes, stirring occasionally. Stir remaining 2 tbsps. margarine into hot rice and arrange into the shape of a ring on a warm serving dish. Spoon chicken livers and sauce into the center of the rice ring. Serve immediately.

— — —

* HOT CHICKEN SANDWICHES *   325° oven

16 slices Pepperidge Farm bread | 3 hardboiled eggs, chopped
(this comes thinly sliced)
2 cups chicken in bite size pieces
⅔ cup mayonnaise

3 hardboiled eggs, chopped
2 tbsps. onion, chopped
1 cup black olives, diced
1 small can mushrooms, drained

Place 8 slices of bread in a baking dish or a jelly roll pan. Mix all of the rest of the ingredients together and spread on bread. Top with the remaining bread. Mix:

1 can cream of chicken soup   1 cup sour cream

Pour over sandwiches. Sprinkle with paprika. Bake in a 325° oven for 20 to 25 minutes. Garnish parsley. Perfect for company luncheons.

— — —

* COUNTRY FRIED CHICKEN *   350° oven

1 (3½ lb.) chicken
½ cup flour
2 tsps. salt

½ tsp. pepper
1 tsp. paprika
6 tbsps. oil

Cut up chicken into serving pieces. Mix the flour and seasonings and coat the chicken. Brown in the oil and transfer to a casserole dish. Add ¾ cup water, cover and bake in a 350° oven for 1 hour or until done.

— — —

* TERIYAKI TURKEY BARBECUE *

1 (28 oz.) frozen white meat
turkey roast
½ cup packed brown sugar
½ cup soy sauce
½ cup water
¼ cup dry sherry

2 tbsps. oil
2 tsps. vinegar
1 tsp. ground ginger
1 clove garlic, minced
1 fresh pineapple, cut in spears

Partially thaw the turkey roast, then cut into 12 slices. Arrange in a shallow dish. In a bowl, mix all ingredients except pineapple. Pour sauce over turkey. Cover and refrigerate for 1 hour. Remove turkey from pan, reserving liquid. Barbecue or grill over medium heat or coals until done, about 25 minutes. Turn and baste often with the marinade. 10 minutes before turkey is done, grill the pineapple spears until golden, turning and basting often with the marinade.

— — —

MEATS AND CASSEROLES

* GOVERNOR'S TENDERLOIN *

1 beef tenderloin
1 tsp. garlic juice
1 tbsp. fines herbes or ground
   rosemary

¼ cup olive oil
¼ cup Broil King

Remove membrane from meat before marinating. Mix together the rest of the ingredients and place together with meat in a strong plastic bag and tie securely. Float bag in a bowl of water to allow tenderizer to reach all parts of the meat. Marinate for 4 hours or overnight. Do not refrigerate as this slows action of marinade. Salt and pepper to taste, broil 5 inches from sides and 2 inches from the oven elements. Serve with justifiable pride to 5 lucky guests.

Note: This recipe was adapted by an engineer-cook from a recipe used by Governor William Quinn's Filipino cook. It makes an ideal meat for guests. Tenderloin, while expensive, entails no waste. The marinade also works very well with budget cuts of meat. Do not substitute any other oil. It is the olive oil which acts as a tenderizer. --Daniel Thompson

— — —

* BUL KOGI *
(Korean Barbecue Steak)

5 lbs. sirloin steak
½ cup soy sauce
¼ cup sugar
2 tbsps. sesame or salad oil

1 clove garlic, minced
4 stalks scallions, minced
1 tsp. MSG

Cut steak across grain into large fillets about an eighth-inch thick. Combine the rest of the ingredients and mix well. Drop each piece of steak in the mixture and marinate for ½ an hour. Broil quickly in the oven or over charcoal.

— — —

* SUNDAY-STYLE SWISS STEAK *

1½ lbs. round or chuck steak,
   about 1 inch thick
2 tbsps. flour
1½ tsps. salt
¼ tsp. pepper

3 tbsps. oil
1 onion, sliced thin
1 can tomato sauce
1 cup water
1 cup frozen peas

Cut steak into 4 pieces. Mix flour, salt and pepper. Pound the flour mixture into steaks. Heat oil in skillet. Saute onion rings until golden, then push to one side. Brown meat slowly on both sides, then cover with onions. Add the tomato sauce and water. Blend, then heat until bubbling. Cover tightly, lower heat and simmer 2 hours or more until meat is very tender. Add the peas 10 minutes before serving.

— — —

* BEEF WITH TOMATOES AND PEPPER *

¼ cup soy sauce	1 clove garlic
1 tbsp. water	2½ cups coarsely diced green peppers
1 tsp. sherry	1 tsp. salt
1½ tsps. cornstarch	½ tsp. pepper
1 lb. flank steak	2 large ripe tomatoes, cut in wedges

Blend soy sauce, water and sherry with the cornstarch. Cut steak into thin slices, add to soy sauce mixture with garlic. Heat oil in skillet. Add peppers and cook over medium heat, stirring constantly, until almost tender. Add beef, salt and pepper and mix well. Cook until meat is tender, about 15 minutes. Stir in tomatoes and serve as soon as tomatoes are heated through.

— — —

* BEEF SUKIYAKI *

4 lbs. top round or sirloin steak	3 bunches watercress or spinach
8 dried mushrooms	½ cup soy sauce
1½ cups water	⅓ cup sake or dry sherry
1 (9 oz.) can bamboo shoots, sliced	¼ cup sugar
2 large onions, sliced	1½ tsps. MSG
1 bunch scallions	⅔ cups beef broth (use bouillon
3 squares tofu, sliced	cubes)

Cut steak against the grain into thin strips, 2 inches long. Soak mushrooms in water until soft. Then discard water, remove stems and slice mushrooms into thin strips. Cut watercress into 2 inch strips. Arrange all the vegetables and meat on 2 large platters. Mix together the rest of the spices and liquids. In a frying pan (electric or hibachi) at the table, heat a little oil. Fry half of the steak, onions and mushrooms. Cook over a brisk fire for a few minutes. Sprinkle with sugar mixture. Use only half as this will make 2 batches. Now add bamboo shoots and cook for 2 more minutes, stirring frequently. Add tofu, watercress and scallions. Baste some sauce over greens. Cover and serve as soon as the watercress wilts. Repeat for a second batch. To be a relaxed hostess, cut all vegetables, slice meat, arrange on platter, cover and refrigerate ahead of time. Mix broth. Let your guests cook the sukiyaki at the table.

— — —

* BEEF DILL POT ROAST *

3 - 4 lbs. beef arm or blade pot roast	3 tbsps. oil
¼ cup flour	1 tsp. dill
1 tsp. salt	¼ cup dill pickle juice
¼ tsp. pepper	¼ cup water
	flour for gravy

continued

Combine flour, salt, pepper and oil. Spread on meat. Sprinkle with dill, juice and water. Cook covered over low heat for 3 to 3½ hours. Remove meat, add flour to drippings slowly to make gravy.

— — —

* CRISP BROCCOLI AND BEEF *

1 small clove garlic	1 lb. round or sirloin steak, cut into
1½ tbsps. oil	thin slices about 1½ inches long
1 lb. fresh broccoli	1 tbsp. soy sauce
¼ cup water	1 tsp. sugar
salt and pepper	1 tbsp. sherry
¼ tsp. MSG	1 tsp. cornstarch
1 tsp. oil	⅓ cup water

Brown garlic in oil in a skillet over high heat. Remove garlic. Chop the broccoli stems diagonally into one-eighth inch slices. Break up the flowerlets. Fry the stems for a few minutes in the hot oil, until they change to a brighter green, stirring constantly. Add flowerlets and stir for a few more minutes. Season with salt, pepper and MSG. Pour into serving dish. Heat 1 tsp. oil in the same pan over high heat. Add beef and sauce, sugar and sherry. Make a paste of the cornstarch and water. Add to meat and stir until sauce thickens. Mix the broccoli and serve.

— — —

* ROMANIAN STUFFED GREEN PEPPER * 350° oven

6 (5 inch) green peppers	1 carrot, grated
boiling water for blanching	½ tsp. salt
1 lb. ground round	dash of pepper
¼ cup uncooked rice or ½ cup	2 eggs
cooked rice or bread crumbs	1 cup water
1 onion, grated	

Sauce: 1 cup tomato puree	3 tbsps. brown sugar
½ cup water	⅛ tsp. paprika
3 tbsps. vinegar or lemon juice	½ cup raisins, optional

Cut away the stem end of the peppers. Remove seeds. Blanch in boiling water and invert to drain while preparing the meat mixture for filling. Combine all ingredients except the water. Mix thoroughly. Stuff pepper compactly and even with the top. Stand upright in a casserole dish and add 1 cup water. Bake in a 350° oven for 45 minutes, covered. Remove cover and increase oven temperature to 400° and cook for 15 minutes more. Combine all of the sauce ingredients and cook in a saucepan until thick, approximately 10 minutes. Use moderate heat. Add to the peppers in casserole and turn off heat. The heat of the oven will be sufficient to lightly brown the tops of the pepper stuffing and to cook the sauce with liquid in the casserole.

— — —

* PINEAPPLE MEAT BALLS *   300° oven

In a large bowl, put 1 egg and ½ cup of milk and mix well. Crumble into this 1 slice of bread and let soak. Then add the following and mix well:

1 lb. ground round	2 tsp. salt
1 lb. ground chuck	grated onion and pepper

Form into walnut size balls and fry in 2 tbsps. oil until brown. Remove to a casserole and pour off remaining fat. In the same pan, add the following:

1 can bouillon	½ cup sugar
1 (no. 2 can) chunk pineapple and juice	2 tbsps. soy sauce
	½ tsp. salt
½ cup chopped green pepper	1 tsp. MSG
¼ cup vinegar	

Simmer together for 15 minutes. Thicken with 2 tbsps. cornstarch mixed with water. Stir until sauce is clear. Pour over meat and bake in a 300° oven for 30 minutes.

— — —

* HAMBURGER SPINACH SCRABBLE *

3 tbsps. butter or margarine	1 cup chopped, well-drained, cooked spinach
2 tbsps. minced onion	
1 lb. hamburger	salt and pepper to taste
½ tsp. MSG	Parmesan cheese
4 eggs, slightly beaten	

Melt the butter in a large skillet. Add the onion, hamburger and MSG. Cook, stirring with a fork until meat is no longer red. Add the spinach and cook until heated thoroughly. Add the eggs, salt and pepper to taste. Stir over low heat until eggs are set. Sprinkle with Parmesan cheese and serve.

— — —

* BEEF PATTIES *

1 lb. ground beef	green onion
2 eggs	watercress
2 tbsps. sesame oil	cabbage
2 tbsps. soy sauce	bean sprouts
2 tbsps. sugar	

Chop enough vegetables to equal 3 cups. Mix with the rest of the ingredients, except the oil, until the mixture is sticky. Shape into thin patties. Heat oil in skillet, fry on low heat until done. Note: different combinations of vegetables may be used for variety.

— — —

* SPEEDY SPAGHETTI *

1 tbsp. oil	½ tsp. dried basil leaves, crushed
⅔ cup chopped onion	¼ tsp. pepper
½ lb. ground beef	4 ozs. uncooked spaghetti
2 (8 oz.) cans tomato sauce	green pepper rings
1½ cups water	parsley
1½ tsps. salt	grated Parmesan cheese
1 tsp. parsley flakes	

Heat oil in skillet, add onion and ground beef. Cook until beef is done. Stir in tomato sauce, water, salt, basil leaves, parsley and pepper. Mix well. Bring mixture to a boil. Break the spaghetti in half and drop it into the sauce a little at a time. Stir to keep spaghetti separated. Cover and simmer for 20 to 25 minutes, stirring occasionally. When done, transfer to a serving platter and garnish with green pepper rings, parsley and cheese.

— — —

* LASAGNE *   375 ° oven

1 lb. hamburger, crumbled	½ tsp. oregano
1 small can tomato paste	8 oz. lasagne noodles
1 can tomato soup	1 pt. cottage cheese, small curd
½ cup catsup	¼ lb. mozzarella cheese
2 tsps. garlic salt	¼ lb. Swiss mild cheese
1½ tsps. salt	½ cup grated Parmesan cheese
¼ tsp. pepper	

Saute hamburger. Add tomato paste, soup, catsup, garlic salt, pepper and oregano and simmer for 20 minutes. While sauce simmers, cook noodles in boiling, salted water for about 15 minutes. Drain noodles. Fill large buttered casserole with alternate layers of noodles, cottage cheese, mozzarella cheese, Swiss mild, meat sauce and Parmesan, ending with meat sauce and Parmesan. Bake uncovered, in a 375 ° oven for 20 minutes.

— — —

* TOAD-IN-THE-HOLE *   400° oven

1 cup flour   pepper
2 eggs   1 lb. Scottish Bangers or
1 cup milk   pork sausage
½ tsp. salt

In a blender, conbine flour, eggs, milk, salt and pepper and mix at high
speed until well blended. Refrigerate for at least 1 hour. Prick each
sausage with a fork and place in a frying pan with 2 tbsps. of water.
Cover and cook over low heat for 2 minutes. Raise heat and uncover.
Cook until well browned. Place sausage in a single layer in a greased
casserole dish. Pour batter over sausage and bake in a 400° oven for 30
minutes. Serve immediately.

— — —

* MOCK CHICKEN CASSEROLE *   350° oven

4 tbsps. butter or margarine   2¼ cups milk
4 tbsps. flour   1 can tuna fish
¼ tsp. pepper   1 (3 oz.) pkg. potato chips, crushed
¼ tsp. salt   ½ cup mushrooms, sliced

Heat butter in saucepan and stir in flour. Blend, then add salt, pepper
and slowly add milk, stirring until smooth. Simmer until sauce begins to
thicken. Add ¾ of the chips and the rest of the ingredients. Pour into a
buttered casserole. Top with the remaining chips. Bake in a 350° oven
for 30 minutes.

— — —

* BEEF STEW (BAKED) *   350° oven

2 lbs. lean stew meat   ½ cup celery, coarsely chopped
1 can tomato soup   1 medium onion, coarsely chopped
1 can cream of mushroom soup   2 carrots, coarsely chopped
½ cup dry wine (vermouth)   1 tbsp. parsley, chopped fine

Mix all of the above in a casserole dish. Cover and bake in a 350° oven
for 2½ hours or until done. After 1 hour of cooking, reduce heat to 275°.

— — —

* LAHAMAGENE *   400° oven
(Meat Pies)

2½ lbs. ground beef or chili   juice of 3 - 4 lemons
1 chopped onion   2 cans refrigerator rolls
1 tsp. each of salt and pepper   butter, melted
¼ cup oil

continued

Fry meat, onion, salt and pepper in oil until done but not brown. Pour liquid off. Squeeze lemon juice all over meat. Form dough into little balls. Dip dough in butter, then form into thin patties. Put some meat in center and roll up like a diploma. Put in buttered pan. Pour remaining butter over the top. Bake in a 400° oven until light brown, about 12 minutes.

— — —

* ISLAND QUICHE *   425° oven

2 (9 inch) pie crusts
2 cups diced ham, crab, shrimp
  or bacon
2 cups cubed sharp cheddar cheese
4 eggs

1½ cups milk plus ⅓ cup milk
½ tsp. salt
pepper to taste
2 tbsps. dry minced onion
mushrooms (optional)

Bake pie crusts for 5 minutes in a 425° oven. Remove from oven. Reduce heat of oven to 375°. Place half of the cheese and ham in each pie crust. In a bowl, mix together eggs, milk, salt and onion. Beat with a fork. Pour half of the mixture in each pie crust. Dot with butter and pepper. Bake for approximately 45 minutes or until the center is firm and not runny. Remove from oven and allow to set for 15 minutes. After this period, quiche may be returned to oven and kept warm in a 150° oven.

— — —

* CHINESE MEAT DISH *   375° oven

1 lb. ground beef
1 pkg. frozen peas
2 cups celery, diced
2 tsps. cream
1 can mushroom soup

½ onion, grated
1¼ tsps. salt
¼ tsp. pepper
1 cup crushed potato chips

Brown beef and line the bottom of a casserole dish. Place peas on top of beef and then the celery. Mix soup, onion, salt, pepper and cream together and pour over peas. Top with potato chips. Bake in a 375° oven for 30 minutes. Serve over rice.

— — —

* STEAMED PORK *

½ lb. ground pork
⅓ lb. chopped shrimp
1 tbsp. cornstarch
1 tbsp. sherry
½ tbsp. soy sauce

1 tsp. salt
1½ tsps. sugar
½ tsp. MSG
½ egg, well beaten

Combine all of the above. Shape into patties 1½ inches round and 1½ inches thick. Place in a serving dish. Set dish on a bowl and place in a pot over 1 inch of hot water. Cover and steam for 20 minutes.

— — —

* CHAR-SIU *
(Chinese Roast Pork)

350° oven

1 (4 - 5 lb.) pork butt
½ cup brown sugar
1 tbsp. salt
¼ cup Hoisin sauce
¼ cup honey
¼ tsp. Chinese Five Spices

2 tsps. soy sauce
2 tbsps. sherry
5 tbsps. red bean curd
1 tsp. MSG
2 tbsps. red food coloring
¾ cup water

Remove meat from pork butt, and cut into strips 1½ inches thick and 4 - 6 inches long. Rub sugar on the pork strips and let stand for 15 minutes. Combine the rest of the ingredients and marinate pork strips in sauce overnight in the refrigerator. Place pork strips on a rack over a pan of water and roast in a 350° oven for 1 hour. Turn pork over after ½ hour, and baste with remaining sauce. Cut pork into eighth inch thick slices. This pork is delicious served plain or stir fried with vegetables as a main dish.

— — —

* QUICK MEXICAN CASSEROLE *

400° oven

2 cups milk
1 can cream of chicken soup
1 can cream of mushroom soup
1 can mushroom pieces

½ can diced chilies, be careful
1 pkg. plain tortilla chips
diced onion, celery and parsley

Saute the diced vegetables in a little margarine. Combine all the ingredients and bake uncovered in a casserole dish in a 400° oven for 20 minutes. Watch out for the chiles. This dish can easily be too hot and spicy to eat.

— — —

* EASY RIBS *

250° oven

3 lbs. spareribs
1 can tomato sauce
1 tbsp. vinegar
3 tbsps. brown sugar

2 tbsps. prepared mustard
dash of Worcestershire sauce
dash of Tabasco
salt and pepper

Boil the spareribs for 30 minutes and then drain. Salt and pepper ribs. Combine the rest of the ingredients and pour over ribs. Bake in a 250° oven until tender.

— — —

* HAWAIIAN SHORT RIBS *

6 lbs. short ribs
1½ cups soy sauce
¼ cup water
½ cup sugar

½ tsp. MSG
1 (1 inch) piece ginger, mashed
3 tbsps. brandy or bourbon
1 clove garlic, mashed

continued

In a large pot, cover short ribs with water and boil for 25 minutes. Remove from heat and let cool. Drain meat and dry. Mix other ingredients in a deep narrow bowl, add short ribs and marinate for 10 to 15 minutes. Grill ribs about 5 inches above hot coals for 15 to 20 minutes or until golden brown and crispy.

— — —

* HAM-APPLE SCALLOP *   375° oven

leftover ham, thinly sliced
equal amount of sliced apples
soft bread crumbs
1½ cups hot water
¼ cup molasses

1 tbsp. vinegar
½ tsp. salt
2 tbsps. sugar
¼ tsp. dry mustard
dash of cloves, ground

Grease a 2-quart casserole and alternate layers of ham, apple and bread. Combine the rest of the ingredients and pour over the ham-apple mixture. Sprinkle with buttered bread crumbs and bake in a 375° oven for 45 minutes.

— — —

* CRISPY ROAST PORK *   425° oven

2 lbs. belly pork
Marinade:
3 tbsps. soy sauce
5 tbsps. Hoisin sauce
2 tbsps. sherry
2 tbsps. sugar

¼ tsp. MSG
¼ tsp. Chinese Five Spices
1¼ inch slice of ginger, crushed

Lightly score pork on meat side. Combine all the marinade ingredients and rub on the meaty side. Do not get any sauce on the skin. Let stand for 15 minutes. Place pork on rack, skin side up. Bake in a 425° oven for 15 minutes, then in a 375° oven for 40 to 50 minutes, or until skin is blistered. Slice and serve.

— — —

* LONG RICE WITH HAM *

2 pkgs. long rice
water
1 large can chicken broth
2 jiggers rum
¼ tsp. saffron
1 tsp. curry powder

¼ tsp. Tabasco sauce
salt and pepper
1 cup chopped green onions
2 cups leftover ham, chopped
1 tsp. fresh ginger

Soak rice in cold water for 10 minutes and then boil for 7 minutes. Drain well, cut into pieces, and boil again in chicken broth. Add rum, saffron, curry powder, Tabasco, salt and pepper to taste. Bring to a boil. Add onion, ham and ginger. Mix well and serve.

— — —

* HAM WITH TROPICAL SAUCE *

1 canned ham, hot or cold
½ cup raisins
1 cup water
1 (6 oz.) can frozen orange juice
1 (8½ oz.) can crush pineapple
½ cup pecan halves

½ cup halved maraschino cherries
1 (1 lb.) can sliced peaches
¼ tsp. cinnamon
¼ tsp. ground cloves
1 tbsp. cornstarch
1 tbsp. lemon juice

Simmer raisins in water for 10 minutes. Combine the rest of the ingredients, except the cornstarch and lemon juice. Add to the raisins and water and simmer for 10 minutes. Blend together the cornstarch and lemon juice. Stir into fruit mixture. Cook, stirring occasionally until sauce is thickened. Spoon some of the sauce over the ham. Serve remaining sauce with the ham.

— — —

* BAKED SPARERIBS AND SAUERKRAUT *   325 ° oven

Parboil ribs for 3 to 4 minutes, then place a layer in the bottom of a baking dish. Cover with rinsed and drained sauerkraut and a layer of sliced onions. Pour barbecue sauce over the top. Repeat layers and cover with foil. Bake in a 325 ° oven for 2 to 2½ hours. Uncover the last ½ hour.

Barbecue Sauce: (mix together)

1 cup catsup
1 scant tbsp. salt
½ tsp. Tabasco sauce
¼ tsp. chili powder

2 cups water
1 tsp. dry mustard
2 tbsps. brown sugar

— — —

* DELUXE HAWAIIAN SPARERIBS *   450 ° oven

2 lbs. spareribs
salt and pepper
2 tbsps. brown sugar
2 tbsps. cornstarch
1 tsp. salt
¼ cup vinegar

¼ cup cold water
1 cup pineapple juice
1 tbsp. soy sauce
2 green peppers, coarsely chopped
1 cup pineapple chunks

Roast spareribs, seasoned with salt and pepper in a 450 ° oven until crisp, about 1 hour. Turn once or twice. Mix brown sugar, cornstarch and salt in a large skillet. Stir in vinegar, water, juice and soy sauce. Cook slowly, stirring vigorously, until juice is transparent. Add green peppers and cook about 3 minutes. Add pineapple chunks and heat through. Place ribs in a serving dish and drizzle sauce over them.

— — —

* CHINESE PORK AND RICE *

⅔ cup uncooked rice (not minute)
½ cup chopped onion
2 stalks celery, cut in diagonal slices
2 tbsps. salad oil

1½ cups boiling water
1 tsp. beef or chicken bouillon
2 tbsps. soy sauce
2 cups chopped, cooked pork
1 medium green pepper, chopped

Cook and stir rice, onion and celery in oil in a large skillet over medium heat until onion is tender and the rice is golden brown. Stir in the remaining ingredients except the green pepper. Heat to boiling, reduce heat and cover. Simmer until rice is tender and liquid is absorbed, about 20 minutes. Stir in green pepper. Cover. Simmer for 10 minutes.

— — —

* PORK ADOBO WITH SPINACH *

6 pork chops, ½ inch thick
2 lbs. fresh spinach
½ cup water
1½ tsps. salt
4 tbsps. vinegar
½ tbsp. paprika

2 cloves garlic, minced
¼ tsp. pepper
1 tsp. ginger, chopped
½ tsp. MSG
2 bay leaves
2 tbsps. sherry

Wash, cut and drain spinach. Set aside. Make a marinade out of the rest of the ingredients. Place chops in marinade and let stand for 1 hour. Pour marinade and pork into a skillet. Cover and simmer for 1 hour. Remove chops to a serving platter. Add spinach to the hot marinade. Cover and simmer for 5 minutes. Spoon spinach around the pork chops.

— — —

* PORK CHOPS AND APPLES *

6 pork chops, ½ inch thick
4 apples, unpared, cored and sliced

¼ cup brown sugar
½ tsp. cinnamon
2 tbsps. butter

Fry pork chops in a frying pan and cook until almost done. Add apples and top with brown sugar and cinnamon. Dot with butter. Cover and simmer until apples are tender.

— — —

* SALMON TOFU LOAF *   350° oven

2 eggs, beaten
¾ cup evaporated milk
1 can mushroom soup
1 block tofu, well drained and
   cubed
1 small can of salmon

1 tbsp. soy sauce
½ cup soft bread crumbs
½ cup chopped onion
2 - 3 green onions, use all
3 tbsps. chopped parsley

Mix all ingredients except tofu. Mix well and then add the tofu. Put into a greased loaf pan and bake in a 350° oven for 1 hour.

– – –

* APRICOT GLAZED PORK CHOPS *

salt
6 pork chops, 1 inch thick
1 (5½ oz.) can apricot nectar

5 tsps. Worcestershire sauce
1 tbsp. cornstarch
⅛ tsp. ground cinnamon

Sprinkle salt lightly on the bottom of a large frying pan. When the pan is hot, add chops and brown well on both sides. Cover tightly, cook over low heat until tender, about 30 minutes. Combine the remaining ingredients. Pour over chops. Cook, uncovered, until chops are glazed and sauce is thickened. Garnish with apricot halves.

– – –

VEGETABLES

* FAR EAST CELERY *

4 cups celery, cut into bite-sized pieces
1 can cream of chicken soup
1 can water chestnuts, sliced thin
1 small jar pimentos, sliced thin

Boil celery for 5 minutes in salted water. Drain. Mix celery with the other ingredients and put in a 1 quart casserole. Sprinkle with ½ cup bread crumbs. Dot with butter. Add ¼ cup slivered almonds. Sprinkle with paprika. Bake in a 350° oven for 35 minutes.

— — —

* NAMASU *

2 cucumbers, sliced thin
½ tsp. salt
¼ cup white vinegar
1½ tbsps. sugar

¼ tsp. MSG
1 tsp. fresh ginger, finely chopped
   (optional)

Sprinkle cucumbers with salt. Let stand for about 20 minutes. Squeeze out the excess water. Mix the rest of the ingredients together and add to the cucumbers. Mix well and chill before serving.

— — —

* DANISH RED CABBAGE *   325° oven

1 medium head red cabbage,
   shredded
4 tbsps. butter
1 tbsp. sugar

1 tsp. salt
⅓ cup water
⅓ cup vinegar
¼ cup red currant jelly

Combine butter, sugar, salt, water and vinegar in a large pot. When it comes to a boil, add shredded cabbage. Toss and bring to a boil. Cover tightly and bake in a 325° oven for 2 hours. Add jelly, stir and cook 10 more minutes.

— — —

* HAWAIIAN COLE SLAW *

1 small head of cabbage
   red or white

3 - 4 tbsps. mayonnaise
1 (12 oz.) can crushed pineapple

Slice cabbage very thin and cut into ½ inch pieces. Place in a bowl. Add pineapple and enough mayonnaise to moisten. Serve cold.

— — —

* PURPLE CABBAGE WITH SWEET-SOUR SAUCE *

1 small onion, sliced
4 tbsps. shortening
1 cup grape juice
1 medium cabbage, sliced thin

2 sour apples, sliced
2 tbsps. salt
4 tbsps. vinegar
2 tbsps. brown sugar

Cook onion in shortening for 3 minutes. Add grape juice, cabbage, apples and salt. Cook until tender, about 30 minutes. Add vinegar and sugar and cook 5 minutes longer.

— — —

* PICKLED VEGETABLES *

2 cups radishes, carrots and/or
   turnips, all thinly sliced
1 tbsp. salt

¼ cup vinegar
¼ cup water
¼ tsp. MSG

continued

Add salt to vegetables. Let stand for ½ hour. Rinse and squeeze out excess water. Add the rest of the ingredients. Let stand until ready to use.

— — —

* CUCUMBERS IN YOGURT *

Peel and thinly slice 3 or 4 cucumbers. Sprinkle with salt, then drain. Make a dressing of 1 cup plain yogurt and 2 tbsps. mayonnaise, garlic powder and salt. Combine cucumbers and yogurt and refrigerate until serving time.

— — —

* FRIED GREEN BEANS *

2 lbs. green beans, washed	1 tsp. salt
2 tbsps. oil	½ tsp. sugar
½ cup water	½ tsp. MSG

Cut off bean tips and discard. Cut beans into 1 inch lengths. Heat oil in a skillet then add beans, stirring briskly. When beans change color, add the rest of the ingredients. Stir until mixed, then cover and simmer for 4 more minutes until liquid is absorbed.

— — —

* EGGPLANT PARMESAN *   350° oven

2 round eggplants, peeled	4 cans tomato paste
flour	6 cups water
salt	2 tsps. oregano
pepper	2 tsps. thyme
4 eggs, beaten	2 tbsps. sugar
½ cup milk	Parmesan cheese
2 cups grated sharp cheddar cheese	

In a saucepan combine tomato paste, water, spices and sugar. Bring to a boil. Simmer until sauce thickens, about an hour. Meanwhile, slice the eggplant in very thin slices. Wet the slices and dip into a mixture of flour, salt and pepper. Then dip into a mixture of beaten egg and milk. Fry in hot oil. Place a layer of fried eggplant in the bottom of a greased casserole or loaf pan. Pour in some sauce to cover, top with grated cheddar cheese and sprinkle with Parmesan cheese. Repeat layers until all ingredients are used. End with cheese on top. Bake in a 350° oven until bubbly, about 30 to 45 minutes.

— — —

* CURRIED AVOCADO *

4 tbsps. butter
5 tbsps. flour
2 cups milk
1½ tsps. salt

½ tsp. pepper
2 - 3 tsps. curry powder
2 cups diced avocados

Melt butter, add flour and stir to make a paste. Stir in milk gradually, cooking until the mixture thickens. Season with the curry powder, salt and pepper. Remove from fire. Add avocados just before serving. Serve with rice and curry condiments such as mango chutney, chopped macadamia nuts, shredded coconut and raisins.

— — —

* HOT SPINACH SALAD *

1 box frozen spinach
1 tbsp. lemon juice
3 tbsps. chicken bouillon
¼ tsp. salt

¼ tsp. Worcestershire sauce
2 drops liquid sugar substitute or
   1 tsp. sugar

Cook spinach according to package directions. While cooking, add the rest of the ingredients. Finish cooking, stirring often. Serve hot.

— — —

* VEGETABLE TEMPURA *

3 - 4 lbs. of assorted fresh
   vegetables such as green beans,
   carrots, eggplant, mushrooms,
   asparagus tips, artichoke hearts,
   etc.
2 cups flour
½ cup cornstarch

1 tsp. baking soda
2 tbsps. baking powder
1 tsp. salt
1 egg, slightly beaten
1½ cups water
oil for frying

Clean and cut the vegetables into 2 inch lengths and bite-sized pieces. Cut into strips whenever possible. Combine flour, soda, baking powder and salt. Stir in egg, then add water and beat. Leave batter lumpy. Dip vegetables into batter and fry in hot oil until golden. Do not overcook. Serve with Tempura sauce.

TEMPURA SAUCE:
¼ cup soy sauce
1 tbsp. lemon juice

½ cup water
½ tsp. MSG

Mix and use as a dip for tempura.

— — —

* VEGETABLE VINAIGRETTE *

1 box frozen asparagus
1 box frozen artichoke hearts
1 cucumber
½ cup olive oil

3 tbsps. vinegar (wine or herb)
½ tsp. salt
pepper

Cook frozen vegetables as packages direct. Drain and cool. Slice cucumber very thin. Mix the vegetables in bowl and pour in the rest of the ingredients. Toss gently. Let stand for ½ hour before serving.

— — —

* VEGETABLES IN WINE SAUCE *

1½ lbs. small white onions
1 tsp. salt
1 cup sliced carrots
1 green pepper, cut into 1 inch
  pieces
1 tsp. salt

¼ cup butter or margarine
¼ cup flour
1¾ cups chicken broth
¾ tsp. nutmeg
¼ tsp. pepper
⅓ cup dry white wine

Place unpeeled onions in a medium saucepan. Cover with water, add salt. Cook until tender, then drain. Slip off outer skins. Place carrots, green pepper and salt in a saucepan. Cover with water. Cook until tender, about 10 minutes. Drain again. Melt butter in a saucepan. Blend in flour. Cook for 1 minute. Add chicken broth, nutmeg and pepper. Cook, stirring constantly until thickened. Boil for 1 minute. Stir in wine and vegetables. Bring to a boil. Lower heat and simmer covered for 10 minutes.

— — —

* GARDEN FRESH OMELET *

Chop 1 onion, 1 green pepper, 1 large tomato, 1 small hot pepper and saute with ground sausage until tender. Add 6 beaten eggs, stirring and cooking until set. Serve with garlic bread.

— — —

* ZUCCHINI CASSEROLE *   350° oven

3 tbsps. olive oil
1 medium onion, thinly sliced
1 lb. ground beef
3 (8 oz.) cans tomato sauce
1 cup Burgundy or red wine
1 tsp. mixed Italian seasoning

dash of garlic powder
1 tbsp. sugar
salt and pepper
6 - 7 (2 lb.) zucchini
Parmesan cheese

Heat oil, add onion and beef. Cook until browned. Add tomato sauce, wine and seasonings. Cover and simmer gently for 1 hour. Wash zucchini and trim the ends. Cook whole in boiling salted water for 15 minutes or until just tender. Drain. When cool, cut lengthwise in halves and arrange cut side up in a single layer in a greased shallow baking dish. Put sauce over zucchini and bake in a 350° oven for 45 minutes. Serve with Parmesan cheese sprinkled over the top. Use as a meal by itself or as a side dish.

— — —

* ZUCCHINI FRITTERS *

Grate 1 large squash to make about 4 cups. Sprinkle 1 tbsp. salt over zucchini and let stand for 10 minutes. Add chopped onion, 2 beaten eggs and 5 tbsps. flour. Drop mix by spoonfuls in hot oil and fry over medium heat until crisp. Serve very hot.

— — —

* PINEAPPLE BAKED BEANS *   400° oven

1 can pineapple slices in syrup,
  drained
1 lb. beans, baked
2 tbsps. brown sugar

1 tbsp. syrup from pineapple slices
1 tbsp. catsup
1 tsp. prepared mustard

Mix all ingredients except pineapple. Bake in a 400° oven for 30 minutes. Top with well-drained pineapple slices and bake 30 minutes more.

— — —

* FRENCH FRIED ONION RINGS *

Slice large peeled onion about ¼ inch thick. Separate rings. Soak rings for 15 minutes in salted milk. Drain and roll in flour. Fry in deep fat until golden brown.

— — —

* BROCCOLI PUDDING *

350° oven

2 lbs. broccoli or 2 boxes frozen
  chopped broccoli
3 tbsps. butter
3 tbsps. flour
1½ cups milk
3 eggs, well beaten

½ tsp. salt
pepper
2 tsps. grated onion
½ cup fine bread crumbs
3 tbsps. grated Parmesan cheese
2 tbsps. melted butter

Chop up fresh broccoli after it is washed. Heat butter and blend in flour. Cook for 2 minutes. Add milk and stir until mixture is thick. Remove from heat. Slowly add eggs, stirring constantly. Add seasonings and broccoli. Mix well and pour into a buttered casserole dish. Cover with a mixture of bread crumbs, butter and cheese. Bake in a 350° oven for 30 minutes.

— — —

* SWEET POTATO WITH PINEAPPLE *   400° oven

6 small sweet potatoes
⅓ as much sliced pineapple as
  potatoes

⅓ cup honey
¼ cup water, hot

Boil potatoes with skins on. When cool, peel and cut into ¼ inch slices. Mix honey and hot water. Just cover the bottom of a baking dish with honey, add potatoes and pineapple. Pour remaining honey mixture on top and bake in a 400° oven for 10 minutes.

— — —

* POTATO SOUFFLE *

350° oven

3 cups mashed potatoes
3 eggs, separated
bread crumbs

melted butter
chopped parsley
salt and pepper

Add beaten egg yolks to potatoes. Beat hard. Add seasonings. Beat egg whites until stiff and fold into potatoes gently. Place in a casserole dish. Sprinkle with bread crumbs and parsley. Pour butter over top. Bake in a 350° oven for 30 minutes . Use as a side dish.

* CHEESE POTATO PUFF *   350° oven

12 medium potatoes
6 tbsps. butter or margarine
2½ cups grated cheddar cheese

1¼ cup milk
1 tsp. salt
2 eggs, beaten

Peel the potatoes if you wish. Cut the potatoes in half and boil in salted water until tender. Drain and mash thoroughly. Add butter, cheese, milk and salt. Beat all together over low heat until butter and cheese are melted. Fold in eggs and pour into a greased oblong baking pan. Bake in in a 350° oven for 30 to 45 minutes until puffy and golden.

— — —

* SAUSAGE STUFFED POTATOES *   400° oven

1 large potato per person
1 tbsp. butter per potato
milk to moisten

salt
3 cooked pupu sausages or chunks of
Portuguese sausage per potato

Scrub each potato and bake whole in a 400° oven until tender, about 1 hour. When done, cut off a lengthwise section and scoop out the insides, being careful not to break the shells. Mash the potato with butter, milk and salt. Beat until fluffy. Pile the mixture back into the shells, leaving the mixture fluffy, not packed. Set the filled shells on a cookie sheet and bake until lightly brown on the top. Tuck the sausage into the top of the potatoes before serving.

— — —

* CANDIED YAMS *   300° oven

4 medium yams
1 cup orange juice
1 tbsp. grated orange rind
½ cup sugar
1 tbsp. cornstarch

½ cup brown sugar, packed
2 tbsps. melted butter
8 unpeeled orange slices
8 maraschino cherries

Boil yams until almost tender. Peel and cut in halves, lengthwise. Place the halves in a buttered baking dish large enough to accommodate them in 1 layer. Mix the remaining ingredients except orange slices and cherries. Pour over yams. Bake in a 300° oven for 1½ hours, basting every ½ hour. To decorate, top each potato half with a cherry topped orange slice about 30 minutes before done. Baste and continue cooking until done.

— — —

* FRIED RICE I *

3 slices bacon, fried
   and broken into pieces

3 eggs, beaten
½ tsp. soy sauce

continued

After the bacon is cooked, remove bacon and pour eggs and soy sauce in with the bacon fat. Cook until mixture is dry, stirring constantly. Remove from pan.

1 tbsp. margarine	½ tsp. salt
4 cups cold cooked rice	¼ tsp. MSG
1 tbsp. soy sauce	¼ lb. luncheon meat, chopped fine

Melt the margarine, then add the rest of the ingredients. Toss lightly to mix. Heat through.

1 bunch watercress

Wash watercress and shake dry. Cut into 1 inch lengths. Cook in a separate covered pot with no water until wilted, about 5 minutes. Add watercress, bacon and eggs to rice. Toss and serve hot.

— — —

* FRIED RICE II *

3 tbsps. oil	sliced assorted vegetables like celery,
2 eggs, beaten	mushrooms, broccoli, waterchest-
¼ cup cooked bacon or ham bits	nuts
½ cup cooked pork, beef, or	2 tbsps. soy sauce
chicken slivers	½ tsp. sugar
½ cup scallions, chopped	¼ tsp. MSG
4 cups cold cooked rice	½ tsp. salt

Heat half of the oil in a large skillet and scramble the eggs. Remove from pan. Add the rest of the oil and fry the meat and scallions. After a few minutes, add rice and vegetables, stirring constantly. Pour in the rest of the ingredients then add the eggs. Heat and serve.

— — —

* RICE SUPREME *

Boil 2 tbsps. rice until tender and dry. Dissolve a quarter of a box of gelatin in a cup of water, add to the hot rice and let cool. Fold in a cup of whipped cream, 2 tbsps. of powdered sugar, 1 tsp. vanilla, 1 tbsp. chopped preserved ginger and let it set in a mold. Serve very cold with whipped cream.

— — —

* RED FLANNEL HASH *

Chop equal parts of cooked potatoes and beets. Add to 2 tbsps. bacon fat or butter in a frying pan. Season well with salt and pepper. Moisten with hot water and cook slowly, covered, then brown quickly. Add a cup of chopped meat if desired.

— — —

* GREEN RICE *

1 cup uncooked rice, cook
½ lb. cheddar cheese, grated
½ cup (small can) evaporated milk
½ cup parsley flakes

½ cup oil
1 small onion, chopped fine
salt and pepper

Combine all of the ingredients in an oblong shallow casserole. Bake in a 350° oven for 45 to 60 minutes or until bubbly. Serve with a simple entree as this is very rich.

— — —

* BITTER MELON AND EGGPLANT *

3 long eggplants
2 bitter melon or ¾ lb. fresh okra
2 cloves garlic, sliced
1 tsp. bagoong sauce

½ cup water
2 medium tomatoes, sliced
¼ cup shrimp
dash of MSG

Wash and slice vegetables. Remove seed from the melon. Cut all vegetables in 2 inch pieces. Mix garlic, bagoong sauce, water, sliced tomatoes and shrimp in a deep pot. Add the melon and eggplant. Cover and simmer until eggplant is cooked, about 5 to 8 minutes. Serve hot.

— — —

* BUTTERY RICE *

1 cup butter (2 sticks)
1 large onion, finely chopped
1 large clove garlic, minced
2 cups raw rice
4 cups boiling water
2 tsps. salt
12 cloves

12 whole cardamon pods
¼ tsp. allspice
1 inch piece stick cinnamon
½ tsp. ground tumeric
¼ cup blanched, slivered almonds
½ cup raisins

Saute onion and garlic in half of the butter in a large skillet for 5 minutes. Add rice and cook 5 minutes more, stirring constantly. Add boiling water and all spices. Cover and simmer 30 minutes until all water is absorbed. Meanwhile, in a separate skillet, melt the rest of the butter. Add almonds and cook, stirring until golden brown. Add raisins. Cook, stirring until raisins puff up. Stir raisin mixture into rice. Serve hot.

— — —

* SPINACH RICE CASSEROLE *   325° oven

1 (10.) pkg. frozen spinach,
   cooked and drained
2 cups cooked rice
½ cup chopped onion
½ cup butter

1 tsp. salt
¼ tsp. pepper
2 eggs, slightly beaten
2 cups milk
1½ cups grated sharp cheese

continued

Saute the onion in butter. Mix all ingredients together and turn into a buttered 1½ quart casserole, uncovered. Bake in a 325° oven for 1 hour and 15 minutes until custard is set.

— — —

* CARROT SOUFFLE *   350° oven

6 medium carrots	¼ tsp. salt
1 cup milk	¼ tsp. pepper
1 small onion, sliced	paprika
½ small bay leaf	nutmeg
⅓ cup butter	cayenne
2 tbsps. flour	3 tbsps. grated Parmesan cheese
3 egg yolks, slightly beaten	3 egg whites

Scrape carrots and cut into ¾ inch slices. Boil in salted water until tender. Drain and place in a generously buttered 2 quart souffle mold. Scald milk with the onion slices and bay leaf. Strain. Heat butter in a larger saucepan, add flour and stir until blended. Slowly add the scalded milk, cook, stirring over moderate heat until mixture is smooth and thickened. Remove from heat, cool slightly. Blend in egg yolks, salt, pepper, paprika, nutmeg and cheese. Beat egg whites until stiff but not dry. Fold into sauce. Pour over carrots and bake in a 350° oven for 35 to 40 minutes.

— — —

BREAD AND PASTRIES

* HAWAIIAN MANGO BREAD *   350° oven

2 cups flour	3 eggs
1¼ cup sugar	¾ cup vegetable oil
½ tsp. salt	½ cup chopped nuts
2 tsps. cinnamon	6 oz. crushed pineapple
2 tsps. baking soda	2 cups diced mango

Sift together all dry ingredients into a large mixing bowl. Mix well and add oil, eggs and pineapple. Beat well. Add mango and nuts. Pour into a well-greased and floured loaf pan and bake at 350° for 40 minutes.

— — —

* QUICK ROLLS WITH PRALINE SAUCE * 375° oven

2 cups flour	2 beaten eggs
2 tbsps. sugar	¼ cup melted butter
2 tsps. baking powder	¼ cup milk
½ tsp. salt	1 tsp. grated orange peel
¼ tsp. nutmeg	oil for frying

Combine dry ingredients in a large mixing bowl and make a well in the center. Mix together eggs, butter, milk and orange peel. Add to dry ingredients and mix until well combined. Cover and chill about 2 hours. Roll out half at a time to ½ inch thickness. Cut dough into 4 inch rounds. Fry in deep hot oil until golden brown, turning once. Drain and serve with Praline Sauce.

Praline Sauce:

1 cup dark corn syrup	½ cup chopped pecans
3 tbsps. brown sugar	¼ tsp. vanilla
3 tbsps. water	

In a saucepan combine first 3 ingredients. Cook and stir over medium heat until mixture boils. Boil for 1 minute and remove from heat. Stir in nuts and vanilla. Drizzle over warm rolls.

— — —

* PEANUT BUTTER BANANA BREAD * 350° oven

1¾ cup flour	⅓ cup margarine
2 tsps. baking powder	⅔ cup sugar
½ tsp. baking soda	2 eggs
½ tsp. salt	1 cup mashed bananas
¾ cup crunchy peanut butter	

Sift together flour, baking powder, baking soda and salt. Cream peanut butter, margarine and sugar together in a large bowl. Add eggs and beat well. Add dry ingredients and banana pulp. Mix thoroughly. Pour into a well-greased loaf pan and bake at 350° for 1 hour.

— — —

* BANANA-DATE BREAD * 350° oven

2½ cups sifted flour	1 cup vegetable oil
2 cups sugar	2½ cups chopped bananas
1 tsp. salt	4 eggs
3 tsps. baking soda	1 cup walnuts, coarsely chopped
1 cup chopped dates	

Mix flour, sugar, salt and baking soda together; add chopped dates (use chopped dates but chop finer) and mix. Mash between fingers any large pieces of dates. Add the rest of the ingredients and mix well until smooth (use mixer). Bake 45 minutes at 350°. Makes 3 loaves.

— — —

* WHOLE WHEAT BANANA BREAD *   350° oven

2 cups bran cereal	1½ tsp. salt
2 cups whole wheat flour	6 large bananas
2 tbsps. baking powder	½ cup milk
1 cup brown sugar	½ cup vegetable oil
½ cup chopped nuts	2 eggs

Mix dry ingredients in a large mixing bowl. Blend bananas, milk, oil and eggs in blender and stir into dry ingredients. Pour into well-greased and floured loaf pans and bake at 350° for 45 minutes. Makes 2 loaves.

— — —

* BANANA-NUT BREAD *   350° oven

2 cups flour	½ cup butter
2½ tsps. baking powder	¾ cup sugar
¼ tsp. baking soda	2 large eggs
¼ tsp. salt	½ cup chopped unsalted macadamia
1 cup mashed bananas	nuts

Sift together flour, baking powder, baking soda and salt. Mash bananas in a separate bowl. Add creamed butter and sugar and mix well. Mix in eggs and dry ingredients and fold in nuts. Pour into well-greased loaf pan and bake at 350° for 50 minutes.

— — —

* PINEAPPLE-NUT BREAD *   350° oven

2½ cups sifted flour	1 cup bran
¾ cup sugar	¾ cup chopped nuts
1½ tsp. salt	1½ cup crushed pineapple
3 tsps. baking powder	1 egg, beaten
½ tsp. baking soda	3 tbsps. melted butter

Sift together flour, sugar, salt, baking powder and baking soda. Combine remaining ingredients and stir into dry ingredients. Pour into well-greased and floured loaf pan and bake for 1½ hours at 350°.

— — —

* ORANGE-NUT BREAD *   350° oven

2 cups flour	2 tbsps. melted butter
½ tsp. salt	1 cup sugar
1 tsp. baking powder	1 egg, beaten
½ tsp. baking soda	1 tsp. vanilla
1 orange	½ cup chopped nuts
boiling water	

Sift dry ingredients together. Grate the orange and squeeze into measur-
continued

ing cup. Add enough boiling water to make a cup. Combine with remaining ingredients and stir until blended. Stir into dry ingredients until mixed. Mix in nuts. Pour into well-greased and floured loaf pan and bake at 350° for 1 hour.

— — —

* PINEAPPLE-COCONUT BREAD *   325° oven

1 (2½ lb.) can crushed pineapple	4 cups flour
1 (10 oz.) can shredded coconut	2 tsps. salt
4 beaten eggs	2 tsps. baking soda
1½ cups sugar	

Mix pineapple, coconut, eggs and sugar with wooden spoon. Sift in remaining dry ingredients and mix well. Pour into well-greased and floured loaf pans. Bake at 325° for 1 hour. Makes 2 loaves.

— — —

* COCONUT BREAD *   350° oven

1¼ cup shortening	1¼ tsp. salt
1½ cup sugar	1½ cup milk
5 medium eggs	3 tsps. coconut extract
5 cups flour	1½ cups coconut, shredded
5 tsps. baking powder	sweetened
1 tsp. baking soda	

Cream shortening and sugar. Add eggs one at a time and beat well. Sift in dry ingredients. Add milk and extract alternately. Mix in coconut. Pour into well-greased and floured loaf pans. Bake at 350° for 1 hour. Makes 4 loaves.

— — —

* COTTAGE CHEESE BREAD *   350° oven

1 cup cottage cheese	2 tsps. dill weed
½ cup warm water	1 tsp. salt
1 package yeast	¼ tsp. baking soda
2 tbsps. sugar	1 egg
2 tbsps. minced onion	2½ cups flour

Dissolve yeast in very warm water in a large mixing bowl and let stand for about 10 minutes. Warm cottgae cheese in saucepan and add to yeast mixture. Add onion, dill, salt, baking soda, egg and sugar, beating all the while. Mix in half the flour until smooth, then mix in remaining flour. Add a little more flour if needed as the moisture of cottage cheese varies. Cover bowl with a dishcloth and set in a warm place. Allow to rise twice its size, punch down and divide into 4 mini-loaf pans, 6 custard cups or 8 large muffin cups (well-greased). Cover and let rise again until double in size. Bake at 350° for 30 minutes, cover with foil and bake for 10 to 15 minutes more.

— — —

* MOLASSES BREAD *   300 ° oven

¾ cup molasses   ¾ cup sugar
1 egg   3 cups whole wheat flour
2 cups milk   1½ tsp. baking soda
½ cup melted shortening   1½ tsp. salt
½ cup white flour   ½ cup cornmeal

Mix molasses, egg, milk and shortening. Sift in dry ingredients and mix well. Pour into well-greased and floured loaf pans. Bake at 300 ° for 65 minutes. Makes 2 loaves.

— — —

* CRANBERRY ORANGE BREAD *   350 ° oven

1 cup cranberries   ½ tsp. salt
2 cups flour   1 orange
1 cup sugar   2 tbsps. vegetable oil
1½ tsp. baking powder   1 egg, beaten
½ tsp. baking soda   ½ cup chopped nuts

Cut cranberries in half. Sift together flour, sugar, baking powder, baking soda and salt. Grate outer rind of orange and squeeze juice from orange. Add enough water to juice to make ¾ cup liquid. Add rind, liquid, oil and egg to dry ingredients and mix thoroughly. Fold in cranberries and nuts. Pour into well-greased loaf pan and bake at 350 ° for 1 hour.

— — —

* MILK BREAD *   400 ° oven

2 cups milk   2 tsps. salt
¼ cup warm water   1 tbsp. shortening
1 cake yeast   6 cups flour
2 tbsps. sugar

Soften yeast in warm water. Scald milk and add sugar, salt and shortening. Cool and add 2 cups of flour. Add softened yeast and mix well. Add enough more flour to make moderately stiff. Turn onto a floured board and knead until smooth, about 5 minutes. Roll into a ball, place in lightly-greased bowl, cover and let rise twice its size. Shape into 2 loaves and place into 2 lightly-greased loaf pans. Allow to rise again twice its size and bake at 400 ° for 50 minutes.

— — —

* PAO DOCE *   350 ° oven
(Portuguese Sweet Bread)

1 large potato   ¼ cup butter
2 tbsps. sugar   3 large eggs
1 pkg. active dry yeast   ¾ cup sugar
¼ cup milk   4 cups flour
1 tsp. salt

continued

Boil potato and save ¼ cup of the water in which it was boiled. Mash potato. Dissolve 2 tbsps. sugar and yeast into the potato water. Stir in mashed potato and allow to rise. Scald milk, add salt and allow to cool. Melt butter. Beat eggs in a large, warm mixing bowl and save aside 1 tbsp. of the beaten eggs. Slowly beat in sugar and melted butter. Combine egg and yeast mixtures. Add one-third of the flour and ¼ cup milk and beat well. Add another third of the flour and beat until blended. Put mixture onto a well-floured cutting board and add the rest of the flour. Knead, folding 85 to 100 times. Place in an oiled bowl and allow to rise twice its size. Punch down and divide into 2 well-greased loaf pans. Let rise again twice its size. Brush loaves with remaining egg mixture. Bake at 350° for 35 to 45 minutes. Makes 2 loaves.

— — —

* PUMPKIN BREAD *   350° oven

3½ cups sifted flour	½ tsp. nutmeg
1½ cups light brown sugar	4 eggs
1½ cups sugar	1 cup vegetable oil
2 tsps. baking soda	⅔ cup water
1½ tsp. salt	2 cups mashed pumpkin
1 tsp. cinnamon	

Combine all dry ingredients in a large mixing bowl. Add eggs, oil, water, and pumpkin. Beat until well mixed. Pour into well-greased loaf pans, sprinkled with brown sugar. Bake at 350° for 1 hour and 15 minutes. Makes 3 loaves.

— — —

* LEMON BREAD *   325° oven

1 tbsp. grated lemon rind	1½ cups sifted flour
⅓ cup melted butter	1 tsp. baking powder
1¼ cups sugar	1 tsp. baking soda
2 eggs	½ cup milk
¼ tsp. almond or vanilla extract	1 tbsp. lemon juice

Blend butter with 1 cup sugar in a large bowl. Add lemon rind and beat in eggs one at a time. Add the extract. Sift dry ingredients together and add to egg mixture alternately with milk. Blend just to mix. Fold in nuts. Pour into a well-greased loaf pan and bake at 325° for 60 to 70 minutes. Mix lemon juice with remaining sugar in a small saucepan. Heat and stir until sugar is dissolved. Spoon the mixture over the hot bread. Cool 10 minutes, remove from pan and store for 24 hours before cutting.

— — —

* BUTTERY CORNBREAD *   350° oven

2 cups milk
4 eggs
1 lb. melted butter
½ cup sugar

4 cups Bisquick
2 tsps. baking powder
6 tbsps. cornmeal

Combine the liquid ingredients. Add to dry ingredients. Mix well.
Bake in a 350° oven for 1 hour.

– – –

* IRISH BARM BRACK *   400° oven

1 pkg. dry yeast
¼ cup warm milk
4 cups flour
3 tbsps. sugar
¼ tsp. cinnamon
¼ tsp. nutmeg
¼ tsp. salt

2 tbsps. butter
1 cup milk
2 eggs
1 cup white raisins
½ cup glazed fruit peel
sugar

Sprinkle the yeast over ¼ cup warm milk. Sift together the dry ingredients into a large bowl, cut in the butter, then combine yeast mixture, milk and eggs. Stir into dry mixture with wooden spoon and knead for 10 minutes. Work in raisins and glazed fruit peel. Let rise until double in bulk. Brush with sugar and place in well-greased loaf pan. Bake at 400° for 1 hour. Serve with Irish coffee.

– – –

* CANADIAN LEMON BREAD *   325° oven

½ cup butter
1 cup sugar
grated rind of 1 lemon
2 eggs

1½ cups flour
1 tsp. baking powder
½ tsp. salt
½ cup milk

Topping (mix together):
¼ cup sugar   juice of 1 lemon

Cream butter and sugar, add lemon rind and eggs, one at a time. Sift together flour, baking powder and salt. Add alternately with milk. Pour into loaf pan and bake at 325° for 1 hour. About 5 minutes before loaf is done, spread with topping.

– – –

* BROWN WALNUT BREAD *   325° oven

1 cup flour	6 oz. evaporated milk
½ cup sugar	½ cup water
2 tsps. baking soda	1 tbsp. vinegar
½ tsp. salt	1 egg, beaten
1½ cups graham flour	1 cup dark molasses
1½ cups chopped walnuts	maple syrup

Sift together flour, sugar, baking soda and salt into a large bowl. Stir in graham flour and 1 cup walnuts. Mix the milk with water and stir in vinegar. Add to the flour mixture. Add the egg and molasses and beat until well mixed. Place into a well-greased loaf pan and bake at 325° for 1 hour and 15 minutes. Cool for 10 minutes. Remove from pan and allow to cool completely. Brush the top with maple syrup and sprinkle with remaining walnuts. Wrap in foil and store for at least 24 hours before serving.

— — —

* BANANA WHEAT GERM MUFFINS *   400° oven

1½ cups sifted flour	¼ cup chopped nuts
3 tsps. baking powder	2 beaten eggs
½ tsp. salt	1 cup mashed bananas
½ cup sugar	½ cup milk
1 cup wheat germ	¼ cup vegetable oil

Sift together flour, sugar, baking powder and salt into a large mixing bowl. Stir in wheat germ and nuts. Add eggs, banana pulp, milk and shortening and mix until dry ingredients are moistened. Spoon into 12 well-greased muffin tins, about two-thirds full. Bake at 400° for 20 to 25 minutes.

— — —

* CHEESY MACADAMIA BISCUITS *   400° oven

1½ cups flour	¼ lb. Swiss cheese, grated
½ tsp. salt	1 egg
½ cup soft butter	⅓ cup chopped macadamia nuts

Sift together flour and salt. Blend butter, cheese and egg. Slowly work in flour and nuts. Mold into a roll 1½ inch in diameter. Wrap in wax paper and chill until firm. Slice into ¼ inch sections. Place onto lightly buttered cookie sheets and bake at 400° for 10 to 15 minutes. Makes 3 dozen biscuits.

— — —

* ORANGE ROLLS *   425° oven

1 cake compressed yeast
¼ cup lukewarm water
¼ cup oil
2 tbsps. sugar
1 egg
1½ tsps. salt

1 tbsp. grated orange rind
3½ cups sifted flour
¾ cup orange juice
sections of 1 orange cut into 1 inch
    pieces

Dissolve yeast in warm water. Add oil, sugar, egg, salt, orange rind and juice. Add flour gradually, beating after each addition. The dough should be soft but not sticky. Turn onto a lightly-floured board and knead until smooth. Place in a greased bowl, cover and let rise in a warm place until double in bulk (abour 1 hour). Roll dough about ½ inch thick and cut with 2½ inch round cutter. Let rest for a few minutes. Shape like Parker House rolls, inserting a piece of orange in the crease of each roll. Place ½ inch apart in 8 inch square pans. Let rise in a warm place until double in bulk. Bake at 425° for 15 to 20 minutes. Brush with butter and while still warm cover generously with Orange Icing.

Orange Icing:
1 tbsp. butter
1 tbsp. lemon juice
1½ cups confectioner's sugar

1 tbsp. orange juice
1 tsp. grated orange rind

Combine butter, lemon, orange juice and orange rind. Heat over boiling water until butter melts. Remove from heat, stir in confectioner's sugar and beat well.

— — —

* QUICK PECAN ROLLS *   325° oven

1 large roll refrigerated biscuits
½ cup chopped pecans
3 tbsps. melted butter

¼ cup brown sugar
¾ tsp. cinnamon

Combine sugar, nuts and cinnamon. Separate biscuits and dip in melted butter. Coat with pecan mixture. Place biscuits in a greased tube pan, overlapping them to form a circle. Bake at 325° for 25 minutes.

— — —

* HOT BUTTERED RUM CRESCENTS *   375° oven

½ cup packed brown sugar
¼ cup chopped nuts
½ tsp. rum flavoring

2 (8 oz.) cans refrigerated crescent
    rolls

Topping:
¼ cup margarine
½ cup packed brown sugar
2 tsps. flour

1 tbsp. milk
½ tsp. rum flavoring

continued

Prepare topping by mixing the ingredients together and bringing to a boil over medium heat. Spoon 2 tbsps. of topping into each of 16 ungreased muffin tins.

Combine ¼ cup brown sugar, chopped nuts and rum flavoring. Separate crescent dough and brush with butter. Sprinkle each with 1 tbsp. of sugar and nut mixture. Roll up, starting at shortest end of triangle. Cut rolls in half crosswise. Place both halves in each muffin cup, cut ends down. Brush tips with melted butter. Bake at 375° until golden brown and invert pan to remove immediately. Serve hot.

— — —

* SHORT'NIN' BREAD *   325° oven

4 cups unbleached flour	1 egg yolk
1 cup light brown sugar	1 tbsp. water
1 lb. butter	

Mix the flour and sugar. Cut the butter into pads over the flour mixture and mix in with fingertips until blended into a paste. Pat on a floured surface to a thickness of about ½ inch. Cut into squares and place onto ungreased cookie sheet. Brush each square with egg blended with 1 tbsp. water. Bake at 325° for 20 to 25 minutes.

— — —

* COCONUT CAKE DOUGHNUTS *

2 eggs	2⅓ cups sifted flour
½ cup sugar	2 tsps. baking powder
¼ cup milk	½ tsp. salt
2 tbsps. vegetable oil	½ cup flaked coconut

Beat eggs with sugar until light. Add milk and oil. Add sifted dry ingredients and coconut. Stir until blended. Chill for several hours. Roll out and cut with doughnut cutter. Fry in deep hot oil until brown on both sides. Drain and sprinkle with sugar.

— — —

* BANANA DOUGHNUTS *

4 cups flour	½ tsp. nutmeg
¾ cup sugar	¼ cup shortening
4½ tsps. baking powder	2 eggs, beaten
1 tsp. salt	1 cup ripe mashed bananas
½ tsp. cinnamon	

Sift together all dry ingredients and cut in shortening until very fine. Add the eggs and bananas and mix thoroughly. Turn dough onto lightly-floured surface. Roll about 3/8 inch thick and cut with a floured doughnut cutter. Fry in oil and serve sugared or plain.

— — —

DESSERTS

* APPLE DESSERT *

1 pkg. yellow or white cake mix
½ cup margarine
1 can coconut flakes
1 (21 oz.) can apple pie filling
½ cup brown sugar

2 apples, peeled, cored, sliced
1 tsp. cinnamon
1 cup sour cream
1 whole egg

CRUST: Cut margarine into dry cake mix until crumbly. Mix with coconut. Press firmly into bottom of an oblong ungreased pan. Bake for 10 minutes.

continued

FILLING: Arrange apple pie slices on the warm crust. Alternate with the fresh apple slices. Mix sugar and cinnamon and sprinkle over the top. If desired, add a few nuts and raisins.

TOPPING: Blend together sour cream and egg and drizzle over top of apples. Return to oven and bake in a 350° oven for 25 minutes or until crust is light brown. Do not overbake.

— — —

Variation to the Apple Dessert:

* CHERRY DESSERT *

CRUST: Use a devil's food cake mix instead of yellow or white.
FILLING: Instead of apples, cinnamon and sugar, use the following:

1 can (21 oz.) cherry pie filling   ½ cup sugar or
½ tsp. almond extract   ½ pkg. cherry Jello

Heat cherry pie filling, extract and sugar (or Jello) until just warm and well-mixed. Spoon over warm crust. Continue with same topping and baking.

— — —

* SUGARLESS APPLE TARTS *

1 (12 oz.) can frozen apple juice   1 tsp. cinnamon
  concentrate   ½ tsp. nutmeg
2 tbsps. butter or margarine   6 - 7 cups thinly sliced tart apples
3 tbsps. quick-cooking tapioca   (about 2½ lbs.)
⅛ tsp. salt

Combine all of the above in a large frying pan. Cover and simmer until apples are tender, about 15 to 20 minutes. Cool, cover and chill for up to 4 days. Use prepared pastry cups or make your own. Spoon 1/3 cup apple filling into each baked tart shell. Garnish each with sweetened whipped cream and sliced nuts.

— — —

* APPLE CHEESE CRISP *   350° oven

6 cups thinly sliced tart apples   ½ cup sugar
½ tsp. cinnamon   ⅔ cup sifted flour
½ tsp. nutmeg   ¼ tsp. salt
1 tbsp. lemon juice   ⅓ cup butter or margarine
½ cup corn syrup   1 cup grated cheddar cheese
½ cup brown sugar

Arrange apple slices in a buttered baking dish. Sprinkle with cinnamon and nutmeg. Pour lemon juice and corn syrup over apples and sprinkle with brown sugar. Combine sugar, flour and salt. Cut in butter until mixture is chunky. Stir in the grated cheese, then top the apples with this crumbly mixture. Bake uncovered in a 350° oven for 1 hour, until apples are tender. Good served with cream.

— — —

* PEACH COBBLER *   325 ° oven

1 tbsp. margarine
1 cup flour
½ tsp. salt
1 tsp. baking powder

1 cup sugar
1 cup milk
1 quart sliced peaches with juice
sugar

Melt margarine in a casserole. Mix all ingredients except peaches. Pour over melted butter. Top with peaches and juice. Sprinkle with sugar and bake in a slow oven for 1 hour or until done.

— — —

* PEACH ALMOND DESSERT *

1 (1 lb. 3 oz.) can sliced peaches,
    drained, reserve 1 cup syrup
2 envelopes unflavored gelatin
½ cup sugar
¼ tsp. salt

1 tsp. vanilla extract
½ tsp. almond extract
4 - 5 ladyfingers, split
1 (3½ oz.) can flaked coconut
1½ cups whipped cream

Crush all but 10 of the peach slices, set aside. Mix gelatin, sugar and salt in a saucepan. Blend in the reserved peach syrup. Place over low heat and stir until gelatin is dissolved, about 3 minutes. Remove from heat and stir in lemon juice and extracts. Mix in the crushed peaches. Chill mixture until it begins to gel. Meanwhile, arrange ladyfingers, rounded side out, around the sides of a lightly buttered 1½ quart mold. Arrange reserved peach slices on the bottom of the mold. When gelatin mixture is of the desired consistency, stir in the coconut. Then fold in the whipped cream. Turn filling into the mold. Chill until firm, about 2 hours. Unmold onto a chilled serving platter. Garnish with mint.

— — —

* GUAVA LEATHER *   175 ° - 200 ° oven

2 lbs. guavas (any kind)
1 cup granulated sugar

extra sugar for dredging

Scoop pulp and seeds into a blender and run until pulp is liquid. Sieve pulp into a kettle and discard seeds. Put guava shells into blender, liquefy, and add to the pulp. Stir in the sugar. Boil gently, stirring to prevent scorching, until thick enough to hold its shape when spread on a greased cookie sheet. Put sheet in a very slow oven (175 ° to 200 °) and dry, leaving oven door ajar. While still warm, cut into 2x2 inch squares, dredge with sugar and roll into logs.

— — —

* BLUEBERRY BUCKLE *   375° oven

¾ cup sugar
¼ cup margarine
1 egg
½ cup milk

2 cups sifted flour
2½ tsps. salt
2 tsps. baking powder
2 cups well-drained blueberries

Mix sugar, margarine and egg. Stir in milk. Sift together the flour, baking powder and salt and add to the sugar mixture. Carefully blend in the blueberries. Pour into an oiled baking dish. Sprinkle the top with a crumb mixture made of the following ingredients:

½ cup sugar
⅛ cup flour

½ tsp. cinnamon
¼ cup soft butter

Bake in a 375° oven for 45 to 60 minutes.

— — —

* BANANAS FLAMBE *   350° oven

4 bananas
½ cup honey
2 tbsps. butter or margarine

½ tsp. each cinnamon, nutmeg,
   ground cloves and mace
½ cup warmed brandy

Slice bananas lengthwise and place in a greased baking dish. Dribble honey over bananas and dot with butter. Sprinkle with spices. Cover with foil and bake in a 350° oven for 10 minutes, until softened, basting with the pan syrup once. Before serving, pour brandy over bananas, light with a match and baste until flame is extinguished.

— — —

* APPLE FRITTERS *

Core and slice tart apples, leaving the skin on. Add cinnamon and nutmeg to biscuit mix and sufficient beer to make a batter. Deep fry or cook over a camp fire on a stick.

— — —

* MELT-IN-YOUR-MOUTH BANANAS *

4 large firm ripe bananas
3 tbsps. butter
2 tbsps. honey
2 tbsps. lemon or lime juice

2 tbsps. rum
1 pint vanilla or macadamia nut
   ice cream

Peel bananas and cut each into 3 chunks. Melt butter in a large skillet and add banana chunks. Drizzle with honey, add juice and rum. Cook over moderately high heat, basting occasionally, until sauce thickens and carmelizes and bananas are lightly browned and sticky. Spoon over ice cream.

— — —

* NICE ICE *

1 pint strawberries
¼ cup sugar

1 cup lemon or lime sherbert
¼ cup good brandy

Mix the strawberries and sugar in a blender until liquidfied. Freeze in ice tray as cubes until firm. Place frozen cubes in the bottom of a blender and add sherbert and brandy. Blend well, then refreeze until ready to use. Serve in sherbert or wine glasses. Garnish with mint or strawberries.

— — —

* PAPAYA MILK SHERBERT *

1½ cups ripe papaya, mashed
3 tbsps. lemon juice
½ cup orange juice

1½ cups milk
1 cup sugar

Blend papaya pulp with fruit juice. Dissolve sugar in milk and add papaya mixture gradually to the milk. Pour into freezer tray. Stir every ½ hour as mixture freezes.

— — —

* BANANA-PINEAPPLE SHERBERT *

½ cup powdered sugar
1½ cups crushed pineapple
1½ cups banana puree
6 tbsps. lemon juice

½ cup orange juice
⅛ tsp. salt
2 egg whites

Dissolve the sugar in the pineapple, then add the other fruits. Freeze in a freezer tray until almost firm. Add the salt to the egg whites and beat until stiff. Add to the fruit ice and put back into freezer, stirring every ½ hour until firm.

— — —

* PEACH MARLOW *

1 cup fresh peaches, mashed
3 tbsps. sugar

20 marshmallows
1 cup heavy cream, whipped

Sprinkle the sugar on the peaches and set aside. Melt marshmallows in ¼ cup water in a double boiler. As soon as marshmallows are melted, add peach pulp and cool. When cold, and slightly stiff, carefully fold in cream. Freeze without stirring.

— — —

* COFFEE CARAMEL SWIRL *

1 cup light corn syrup	2 tsps. vanilla
few grains of salt	½ cup coffee, double strength
2 eggs, well beaten	2 tbsps. butter
2 tbsps. cornstarch	½ cup dark corn syrup
1½ cups milk	1 tbsp. cornstarch
1 cup whipping cream	1 tbsp. water

Stir light corn syrup and salt into eggs. Blend cornstarch with a small amount of milk. Combine with egg mixture and remaining milk in a double boiler and cook, stirring constantly, until thickened. Cool. Whip cream to custard like consistency. Add vanilla and fold into cooked mixture. Pour into refrigerator tray and freeze until almost firm. To swirl, combine coffee, butter and corn syrup over low heat. Stir constantly until smooth. Blend cornstarch and water, then add to coffee mixture and continue to cook until smooth and thickened. Cool. Remove tray from freezer and stir ice cream until smooth, then draw spoonfuls of the dark syrup mixture lengthwise and then crosswise through the stirred ice cream. Return to freezer and continue freezing.

— — —

* KONA COFFEE CUSTARD *   350° oven

2½ cups milk	4 eggs
½ cup strong Kona coffee or,	½ cup sugar
1 heaping tbsp. instant Kona	pinch of salt
coffee	

Add the coffee to the milk and scald. Stir occasionally. Beat eggs until lemon-colored. Slowly add the sugar and the salt. Beat until blended. Add coffee-milk gradually to the egg mixture and mix well. Pour into a large buttered mold or 8 individual molds. Set the mold or molds in a pan of hot water and bake in a 350° oven for about 30 minutes, or until the custard is firm. Remove from pan, cool, then chill. Good served with whipped cream.

— — —

* FROZEN HEAVEN *

12 marshmallows	2 bananas, mashed
¼ cup pineapple juice	1 tbsp. lemon juice
1 cup heavy cream, whipped	½ cup maraschino cherries
½ cup orange sections	¼ cup chopped nuts
1 cup crushed pineapple, drained	¾ cup macaroon crumbs

Cut marshmallows into small pieces. Heat in pineapple juice until marsh-mallows dissolve. Remove from heat and beat until cool. Add whipped cream and beat again. Fold in well-drained orange sections, pineapple, banana pulp mixed with lemon juice, cherries, nuts and macaroon crumbs. Turn into refrigerator tray and freeze without stirring. If de-sired, line the tray with split ladyfingers before pouring in fruit.

— — —

* RICE PUDDING *   300° oven

1½ pints milk	dash of salt
3 tbsps. cooked rice	butter
2 tbsps. sugar	vanilla
1 cup raisins	

Combine milk, rice, sugar and raisins in deep casserole dish. Add dash of salt and vanilla. Dot with butter. Cook in a 300° oven for 2 - 3 hours until firm. May be served with Poha Sauce.

— — —

* POHA SAUCE FOR BREAD OR RICE PUDDINGS *

3 cups diced pohas	1½ cups pineapple juice
1⅞ cups sugar	½ tsp. vanilla
2 tbsps. cornstarch	1 tbsp. butter
¼ tsp. salt	

Add ½ of the sugar to the pohas and allow to stand for 15 minutes. Add pineapple juice and bring to the boiling point. Mix remaining sugar, salt and cornstarch together thoroughly and add to hot liquid, stirring co constantly. Boil for 5 minutes, remove from heat and add butter and vanilla.

— — —

* BREAD PUDDING *   350° oven

4 cups scalded milk	4 eggs, slightly beaten
¾ cup sugar	1 tsp. vanilla
1 tbsp. butter	2 cups dry bread cubes
¼ tsp. salt	

Soak bread in milk for 5 minutes. Add butter, salt and sugar. Pour in
continued

eggs slowly and stir. Add vanilla. Grease a baking dish and place in a shallow pan with water. Pour pudding into greased pan and bake in a 350° oven for about 1 hour until firm.

— — —

* LEMON ZABAGLIONE *

6 egg yolks
½ cup sugar
1 tsp. freshly grated lemon peel

1 tsp. freshly squeezed lemon juice
⅓ cup marsala or sherry

Beat egg yolks in the top of a double boiler with a rotary beater or wire whisk until foamy. Beat in sugar, lemon peel and lemon juice. Place over simmering, not boiling water. Mix in marsala or sherry slowly, beating constantly with a rotary beater or wire whisk until smooth, pale and thick, about 12 minutes. Mixture should stand in soft mounds. Serve immediately in shallow, stemmed glasses. Garnish with grated lemon peel.

— — —

* ORANGE CAKE TOP PUDDING *   350° oven

¼ cup sifted flour
1 cup sugar
¼ tsp. salt
1 tbsp. grated orange peel

½ cup orange juice
2 egg yolks
¾ cup milk
2 egg whites

Sift flour, sugar and salt together. Stir in orange peel and juice, egg yolks, and milk. Blend well. Beat egg whites until stiff but not dry. Pour orange mixture onto beaten whites and fold gently to blend. Pour into greased, 1 quart baking dish. Set dish in a large pan and pour in hot water to equal 1 inch. Bake in a 350° oven for 50 minutes. Serve warm garnished with halved orange slices, if desired. Pudding will fall slightly as it cools.

— — —

* BANANA COCONUT CUSTARD *   300° - 325° oven

2 cups milk
2 eggs
4 tbsps. sugar
pinch of salt

¾ cup grated coconut
1 cup sliced ripe bananas
¼ tsp. vanilla

Beat eggs slightly, add other ingredients. Pour into a baking dish and bake in a 300° to 325° oven for 1 hour.

* LEMON SPONGE PUDDING *

2 cups milk	1 envelope unflavored gelatin
3 eggs yolks, lightly beaten	¼ cup lemon juice
½ cup sugar	2 egg whites
1 tbsp. cornstarch	⅓ cup sugar
3 tbsps. water	1 cup heavy cream

Scald the milk. Cool slightly. Mix egg yolks with sugar and cornstarch in the top half of a double boiler. Place over hot but not boiling water. Add the scalded milk, beating constantly. Cook, stirring frequently, until custard thickens and coats the spoon.

Sprinkle water over gelatin to soften and stir into warm custard. Cool custard to room temperature. Stir in the lemon juice. Beat egg whites until frothy, then slowly beat in the sugar, a little at a time, beating after each addition. Continue beating to a stiff and shiny meringue.

Beat cream until stiff. Fold first meringue and then the cream into the custard. Pour into molds rinsed with cold water. Refrigerate until firm.

— — —

* BANANA MOUSSE *

¾ cup evaporated milk or	⅓ cup boiling water
whipping cream	⅓ cup mashed bananas
12 marshmallows	2 tbsps. lemon juice

If evaporated milk is used, place can in boiling water and simmer for 20 minutes. Chill evaporated milk or whipping cream thoroughly and whip with an egg beater. Melt marshmallows in boiling water. Cool. Add banana pulp and lemon juice. When the mixture begins to set, fold in whipped milk or cream. Freeze in refrigerator trays.

— — —

* BROWNIE PUDDING *   350° oven

¼ cup ground chocolate	½ cup milk
1 cup sifted flour	2 tbsps. melted butter
1½ tsps. baking powder	1 tsp. vanilla
¼ tsp. salt	½ cup chopped nuts
⅓ cup sugar	

Sift chocolate, flour, baking powder, salt and sugar into a greased baking dish. Stir in milk, butter, vanilla and nuts. Mix just enough to blend the ingredients. Sprinkle with the following topping:

⅓ cup white sugar	¼ tsp. salt
⅓ cup brown sugar	½ tsp. vanilla
¼ cup ground chocolate	

continued

Mix together and sprinkle on the flour mixture. Pour 1½ cups boiling water over the mixture. Do not stir after adding the water. Bake in a 350 ° oven for 45 minutes.

— — —

* HAUPIA *
(Coconut Pudding)

6 cups grated coconut (2 coconuts) for soft pudding: 3 tbsps. cornstarch
2 cups boiling water   for firm pudding: 6 tbsps. cornstarch
3½ tbsps. sugar

Pour boiling water over coconut and allow to stand for 15 minutes. Strain through double thickness of cheesecloth, squeezing out just as much of the milk as possible, about 3 cups. If not 3 cups, add milk poured from the coconut to equal 3 cups. Mix cornstarch with sugar and add sufficient coconut milk to make a smooth paste. Heat remaining milk to boiling and slowly stir in cornstarch paste. Boil until it thickens. Pour into mold and allow to cool. Cut into squares and serve on squares of ti leaves.

— — —

* BAKED CUSTARD WITH SLICED MANGO *   300 ° oven

2 cups milk   ¼ tsp. vanilla
2 eggs   1 cup sliced ripe mangoes
¼ cup sugar   ⅛ tsp. salt

Heat milk to the simmering point, add sugar and salt. Beat the eggs just enough to mix well then slowly add to the hot milk. Place mango slices in the bottom of custard cups or a baking dish. Pour hot custard on mangoes, set dishes in a pan of water and bake in a 300 ° oven for 1 hour. To test for doneness, insert a knife into center of custard. When the knife blade comes out clean, cool and serve.

— — —

* SWEET RICE FRITTERS WITH LEMON SAUCE *

3 cups cold cooked rice
½ cup powdered sugar
grated rind of 1 lemon
½ cup chopped almonds

½ tsp. cinnamon
1 egg, well-beaten
6 tbsps. butter

Combine rice, sugar, lemon rind, almonds and cinnamon in a large bowl. Add egg and mix well. Shape into small rolls, then flatten slightly. Place on a platter and chill well. Melt 3 tbsps. butter in a large skillet over medium heat. Add ½ of the rice rolls and cook until lightly browned, turning once. Drain on paper towels. Melt remaining butter, then cook the rest of the rolls. Sift additional powdered sugar over cooked rolls generously, then place on a serving dish. Serve with a bowl of lemon sauce.

Lemon Sauce:
⅓ cup sugar
2 tbsps. cornstarch
⅓ cup lemon juice
1¼ cups water

½ tsp. grated lemon rind
pinch of salt
¼ cup butter

Combine sugar and cornstarch in a small saucepan. Stir in the lemon juice and water, then add rind and salt. Place over medium heat and cook, stirring constantly until thickened and clear. Remove from heat and stir in the butter. Serve with Rice Fritters.

— — —

* ROYAL DELIGHT *

1 cup whipping cream
¼ cup powdered sugar
8 large or 32 mini-marshmallows
½ cup shredded coconut

1½ cups ripe papaya cubes
½ cup diced orange
2 tsps. lemon juice

Chill and whip the cream. Add sugar and marshmallows. (Cut large marshmallows into quarters.) Fold in papaya, lemon juice, orange and coconut. Pour into individual serving dishes. Chill and then garnish with coconut and maraschino cherry before serving.

— — —

* APRICOT BARS *   350° oven

⅔ cup dried apricots
½ cup soft butter
¼ cup sugar
1⅓ cups sifted flour
1 tsp. baking powder
¼ tsp. salt

1 cup brown sugar, packed
2 eggs
1 tsp. vanilla
½ cup chopped nuts
confectioners' sugar, optional

continued

Rinse apricots, cover with water, stew for 10 minutes, cool and chop, after draining. Mix until crumbly, the butter, sugar and 1 cup of the flour. Pack into a square baking pan. Bake in a 350° oven for 25 minutes, or until lightly brown. Beat eggs, add brown sugar gradually, then add 1/3 cup flour, baking powder and salt. Mix in vanilla, nuts and apricots. Spread on baked layer. Bake for 30 minutes more. Cool in pan, then cut into bars. Roll in confectioners' sugar.

— — —

* SCHOKOLADE PUDDING *   350° oven

5 tbsps. butter or margarine
5 tbsps. melted baking chocolate
5 tbsps. sugar

4 egg yolks, beaten
5 tbsps. ground almonds
4 egg whites, beaten

Mix all ingredients except egg whites. Fold these in last. Grease a small tube pan, set pan in hot water in oven, fill with mixture, after adding beaten egg whites. Bake in a 350° oven for 30 to 40 minutes. Invert when done and fill center with ice cream or whipped cream.

— — —

* WHEAT GERM BARS *   350° oven

2 cups graham cracker crumbs
½ cup wheat germ
½ cup chopped walnuts
1 can condensed milk

1 pkg. chocolate chips or candied
fruit
1 tsp. vanilla

Mix all ingredients together and spread in a baking pan. Bake in a 350° oven for 20 to 25 minutes.

— — —

* LOW-CAL COOKIES *   325° oven

1 cup margarine
½ cup sugar
1 egg

1 tsp. vanilla
2½ cups flour

Cream margarine and sugar. Beat in egg, vanilla amd flour. Form small balls and flatten with base of a glass that has been greased and sugared. These can also be flattened by criss-crossing with the tines of a fork. The dough is a firm one and works well with a cookie stamp. They resemble shortbread but are not as rich. Bake in a 325° oven for 12 minutes.

— — —

* ROCKY ROAD BARS *

10 marshmallows, quartered   ½ lb. sweet milk chocolate
½ cup broken walnuts

Line a 9x5 inch loaf pan with waxed paper. Arrange marshmallows in the bottom. Fill in spaces with the walnuts. Heat the chocolate over hot water in a double boiler until partially melted. Remove from heat and stir until melted. Pour over marshmallows. Cool until hardened, then cut into bars.

— — —

* PINEAPPLE OR CHERRY FRITTERS *

Batter:
1½ cups flour   1 tbsp. melted butter
½ tsp. salt   1 egg white, stiffly beaten
⅔ cup beer

Sift flour and salt together into a large bowl, then stir in the beer until smooth. Do not beat. Add enough lukewarm water to make a thick batter, then stir in the butter. Use within 30 minutes. Just before ready to use, stir in beaten egg white.
PINEAPPLE: Use 2 (1 lb.) cans pineapple sticks or fresh pineapple spears. Drain the pineapple and place on paper towels. Dip pineapple spears, one at a time into the batter. Shake off the excess. Drop into hot oil and fry until golden brown on all sides. Remove and drain on more paper towels.
CHERRIES: Use 2 lbs. of fresh cherries with the stems still on. Hold the stem and dip into batter and drop into hot oil. Remove with a slotted spoon.

— — —

* WHISKEY BALLS *

3 cups ground vanilla wafers   ½ cup bourbon
1 cup ground nuts   confectioner's sugar
3 tbsps. light corn syrup

Mix all ingredients. Pinch off and roll into balls the size of a large cherry. Roll in confectioner's sugar.

— — —

* ALMOND COOKIES *   300° oven

3 cups flour   1 cup shortening
½ tsp. salt   1 egg
1 cup sugar   1 tsp. almond extract
½ tsp. soda   almonds

continued

Mix dry ingredients. Cut in shortening and add unbeaten egg and extract. Knead until everything is mixed. Break off dough to size of an egg and shape into circles 1 inch in diameter. Place ½ inch apart with an almond on top of each. Bake in a 300 ° oven for 20 minutes. Makes 5 dozen.

— — —

* CHINESE ALMOND COOKIES * 375 ° oven

1 cup rice flour
¾ cup powdered sugar
¼ tsp. salt
½ cup finely ground, blanched
  almonds

6 tbsps. peanut oil
1 well-beaten egg
1 tsp. almond extract
whole blanched almonds

Sift together the dry ingredients, including the almonds. Add the peanut oil. Stir in the egg and the extract. Roll out about ¼ inch thick. Cut into small rounds. Press a whole blanched almond in the center of each. Bake in a 375 ° oven for 15 minutes.

— — —

* CHINESE PRETZELS *

1¾ cups cornstarch
½ cup sugar
1 cup flour
⅛ tsp. salt
¼ cup evaporated milk

1¼ cups water
1 egg, beaten
oil for deep frying
rosette iron

Sift together dry ingredients. Blend milk, water and egg. Combine and mix all of the ingredients until batter is smooth. Heat the head of the rosette iron in the hot oil, and dip into the batter. Be sure not to let the batter run over the top of the iron, for it will be difficult to remove the cookies when cooked. Cook batter on rosette iron in hot oil. Cook pretzels until golden brown. Drain and let cool. Store in airtight containers.

— — —

* BANANA DROP COOKIES *   400° oven

1¼ cups sugar
⅔ cup shortening
1 tsp. vanilla
2 eggs, unbeaten
1 cup ripe mashed bananas
  (about 3)

2¼ cups sifted flour
2 tsps. baking powder
¼ tsp. soda
½ tsp. salt
1 cup chopped macadamia nuts
1 bag semi-sweet chocolate chips

Cream sugar, shortening and vanilla until light and fluffy. Add eggs and beat well. Stir in mashed bananas. Sift flour with baking powder, soda and salt and add to the banana mixture. Mix well. Stir in nuts and chocolate chips. Chill for 30 minutes. Drop by tsps. 2 inches apart on greased cookie sheets. Bake in a 400° oven for 10 to 12 minutes. Makes 5 dozen.

— — —

* CHOCOLATE SNOWBALLS *   350° oven

2 cups sifted flour
½ tsp. salt
¾ cup butter
½ cup sugar
2 tsps. vanilla

1 egg
1 cup chopped nuts
1 (6 oz.) pkg. semi-sweet chocolate
  chips

Sift together flour and salt. Set aside. Blend the butter, sugar and vanilla. Beat in the egg. Stir in the flour mixture, add nuts and chocolate. Shape into 1 inch balls. Place on an ungreased cookie sheet and bake in a 350° oven for 15 to 20 minutes. Cool slightly. Roll in confectioners' sugar. Makes 6 dozen.

— — —

* CHOCOLATE CINNAMON PUFFS *   350° oven

2 cups flour, sifted
1 tsp. baking powder
1 cup sugar
3 tsps. cinnamon
½ cup soft butter
½ cup soft shortening
1 egg yolk

1 tsp. shredded orange rind
1 (6 oz.) pkg. semi-sweet chocolate
  chips
½ cup chopped nuts
1 egg white, stiffly beaten
⅔ cup sugar
2 tsps. cinnamon

Sift together flour, baking powder, sugar and cinnamon. Add soft butter, shortening, egg yolk and orange rind. Mix well. Stir in chocolate chips and nuts. Shape into 1 inch balls. Dip into egg white, then roll in a mixture of sugar and cinnamon. Place on a greased cookie sheet and bake in a 350° oven for 15 to 20 minutes. Makes 5 dozen cookies.

— — —

* BUTTER COOKIES *   375° oven

1 cup butter
1 cup sugar
1 cup brown sugar
1 tsp. vanilla
1 egg

½ tsp. salt
1 tsp. soda
2 cups flour
1 cup mashed potato flakes
1 cup flaked coconut

Cream butter, sugar, brown sugar and vanilla together. Beat in egg, then add remaining ingredients. Shape into 1 inch balls, put on ungreased cookie sheets, then flatten with the bottom of a glass that has been dipped in granulated sugar. Bake in a 375° oven for 6 to 8 minutes or until golden brown. Makes 5 dozen.

— — —

* YAK-KWA *
(Korean Holiday Cookies)

1 cup sugar
¼ cup water
½ cup honey
2½ cups sifted flour

¼ cup oil
¼ cup whiskey
¼ cup finely chopped almonds

Heat sugar with water until sugar dissolves. Add honey and stir until completely mixed. Put flour in a large mixing bowl. Add oil, whiskey and ¼ cup of the warm sugar mixture. Mix thoroughly. The texture should be similar to pie crust dough. Roll dough to ¼ inch thick. Cut into 1 inch squares or triangles. Fry in deep hot oil until brown. Drain on paper towels. While cookies are still warm, soak in the remaining sugar syrup for 2 to 3 minutes each. Roll in finely chopped nuts. Cool. Makes 2 to 3 dozen.

— — —

* POTATO CHIP COOKIES *   350° oven

1 cup shortening
1 cup granulated sugar
2 eggs
2 cups sifted flour

1 tsp. baking soda
1 cup brown sugar, firmly packed
2 cups crushed potato chips
1 cup chopped nuts

Cream shortening with sugar until light and fluffy. Add eggs 1 at a time, beating after each addition. Add dry ingredients and mix until smooth. Add potato chips and nuts and blend. Drop by tsps. onto ungreased cookie sheets. Bake in a 350° oven for 7 to 8 minutes or until lightly browned. Makes 6 dozen.

— — —

* SESAME COOKIES *   350° oven

¾ cup sugar
½ cup butter or margarine
1 egg
½ cup sesame seeds

2 cups flour
1 tsp. baking powder
½ tsp. salt
toasted sesame seeds

Cream together the sugar and butter. Beat in egg and then add sesame seeds. Stir together flour, baking powder and salt. Stir into creamed mixture. Shape into a 8x2 inch round log. Wrap in waxed paper and chill at least 2 hours until firm. Cut into ¼ inch slices. Place on an ungreased cookie sheet and press toasted sesame seeds onto the top of each cookie. Bake in a 350° oven for 12 to 15 minutes. Makes 3 dozen.

— — —

ORANGE CHOCOLATE CHIPPERS *   350° oven

Cream together:
1 cup shortening
1 cup sugar
1 (3 oz.) pkg. softened cream cheese
Add:
2 eggs
2 tbsps. grated orange peel
2 tsps. vanilla

Then add:
2 cups sifted flour
1 tsp. salt

Stir in:
¾ to 1 cup chocolate chips

Drop from a tsp. 2 inches apart on a lightly greased cookie sheet. Bake in a 350° oven for 12 minutes or until done. Cool slightly before removing from pan. Makes about 4 dozen cookies.

— — —

* SALLY'S SUGAR COOKIES *

1 cup sugar
⅔ cup butter
1 egg, beaten
½ cup buttermilk

½ tsp. vanilla
2½ cups flour
½ tsp. baking soda
½ tsp. salt

Cream together the sugar, butter and egg. Sift the dry ingredients together. Add the buttermilk and vanilla to the creamed mixture and then add the dry ingredients. Mix well and then chill overnight. Roll out 1/8 inch thick and cut with a cookie cutter. Bake on a greased pan in a 350° oven until lightly browned, about 12 minutes. Part of this recipe may be used later by storing in the coldest part of the refrigerator. Makes 3 dozen thick and soft cookies.

— — —

* SHORTBREAD COOKIES *   300° oven

1 lb. butter (or ½ margarine
    and ½ butter)

1 ⅓ cups sugar
5 cups flour

continued

Cream butter and sugar, then add flour, 1 cup at a time. Mix well. Pat into jelly roll pan with sides, ¼ inch thick. Bake in a 300 ° oven until light brown. Cut into squares while still warm.

— — —

* GUAVA CRISPIES *   350 ° oven

¼ cup butter
⅓ cup guava jelly
2 tbsps. lemon juice
2 tbsps. sugar
¼ tsp. salt
1 egg yolk, slightly beaten
¼ cup chopped macadamia nuts

1 cup flour
½ tsp. salt
½ tsp. soda
½ cup brown sugar
½ cup butter
1 cup quick oats

Combine butter, guava jelly, lemon juice, sugar and salt in the top of a double boiler. Heat until the guava jelly has dissolved. Stir a part of this into slightly beaten yolk, then return the egg mixture to the rest of the jelly mixture. Heat and stir until the mixture thickens. Add nuts. Remove from heat and cool.
Sift flour, salt and soda over the butter and sugar. Cut together with 2 knives until coarse crumbs form. Add oatmeal and mix well. Pat half of the mixture into the bottom of a 9 inch square pan. Spread guava mixture on top and sprinkle remaining oatmeal mixture on top. Bake in a 350 ° oven for 25 minutes. Cool and cut into squares. Makes 3 dozen.

— — —

* PUMPKIN COOKIES *   375 ° oven

½ cup shortening
1¼ cups brown sugar
2 eggs
1 tsp. vanilla
1½ cups pumpkin
2½ cups flour

4 tsps. baking powder
½ tsp. salt
½ tsp. cinnamon
½ tsp. nutmeg
1 cup raisins
1 cup chopped nuts

Cream together the shortening and brown sugar. Beat in eggs, then add vanilla and pumpkin. Sift together the dry ingredients, then blend into sugar mixture. Stir in raisins and nuts. Spoon onto greased cookie sheets and bake in a 375 ° oven for 15 minutes. Makes 5 dozen.

— — —

* CHINESE CHEWS *   375 ° oven

½ cup soft butter
1 cup flour
¼ cup powdered sugar
2 eggs, beaten
1½ cups brown sugar
2 tbsps. flour

1 cup chopped nuts
¾ cup shredded coconut
¼ tsp. baking powder
1¼ tsps. salt
1 tsp. vanilla
¼ cup chopped dates, optional

Mix the first 3 ingredients with your fingers. With the heel of your hand, spread in a thin layer in an oblong pan. Bake in a 375 ° oven for 12 to 15 minutes. Combine the rest of the ingredients and spread over the baked base. Bake for another 20 minutes. Cool in the pan and then cut into squares.

— — —

* JAVANESE COOKIES *   300 ° oven

½ lb. butter
¾ cup sugar

2 cups flour
1 cup grated coconut

Cream butter and sugar together. Add dry ingredients. Shape into 2 rolls and wrap in waxed paper. Place in refrigerator until firm. Cut into ¼ inch slices and bake in a 300 ° oven for 30 minutes. Sprinkle with powdered sugar while still warm or serve plain.

— — —

* COCONUT LAYER COOKIES *   375 ° oven

½ cup butter or margarine
1 cup flour
1½ cups brown sugar
2 eggs
2 tbsps. flour

¼ tsp. baking powder
½ tsp. salt
1 cup finely chopped nuts
1 cup coconut, shredded
1 tsp. vanilla

Work the butter into the flour until smooth. Pat into a thin layer in the bottom of a rectangular baking pan. Bake in a 375 ° oven until a delicate brown. Top with coconut mixture made by combining the sugar and eggs, then adding the flour, baking powder and salt that have been sifted together. Then add the nuts, coconut and vanilla. Spread on top of baked layer. Bake again for 20 minutes. Cool cookies, then spread with the following icing. Cut into squares. Makes 2 dozen.

Icing:
2 tbsps. butter or margarine
1½ cups powdered sugar

1 tbsp. lemon juice
2 tbsps. orange juice

— — —

* PECAN CRISPIES *   375° oven

½ cup butter
¾ cup plus 2 tbsps. brown sugar,
  packed
1 egg
¼ tsp. vanilla

¼ tsp. salt
1½ cups flour
1½ tsps. baking powder
36 pecan halves

Cream butter and sugar together. Add egg and flavorings and beat well. Mix in the dry ingredients. Roll into balls, the size of walnuts and place on an ungreased cookie sheet. Press 1 pecan half into the center of each cookie. Bake in a 375° oven for 10 to 12 minutes. Cool. Makes 3 dozen.

— — —

* GINGER CREAMS *   375° oven

1 cup sugar
1 cup warm water
4½ cups sifted flour
1 tbsp. ground ginger
3 level tsps. baking soda

1 tsp. cinnamon
½ tsp. salt
little less than a cup of melted
  shortening
1 cup light molasses

Mix all ingredients together. Bake a few minutes in a 375° oven and then turn down oven to 350°. Bake until cookies spring back when tested by pressing lightly with a finger. Frost with the following: Frosting:
Grate rind and juice of ½ of a medium orange. Mix with enough powdered sugar and water to make a thick frosting. Place a dab on each hot cookie when they come out of the oven. The frosting will spread over each cookie as it melts. Makes 2 dozen.

— — —

* CRISP MACADAMIA WAFERS *   350° oven

½ cup butter
½ cup shortening
2½ cups powdered sugar
2 medium eggs

2½ cups flour
¼ tsp. salt
½ tsp. baking soda
1 cup macadamia nuts, chopped

Thoroughly cream butter and shortening with sugar. Add eggs 1 at a time and beat well. Add sifted dry ingredients and then add nuts. Drop by tsps. on greased cookie sheets. Bake in a 350° oven for 10 to 12 minutes. Makes 5 dozen.

— — —

* COCONUT-MACADAMIA NUT BARS *   350° oven

½ cup butter
½ cup brown sugar
1 egg
1¼ cups sifted flour
¼ tsp. salt
2 eggs
1 cup brown sugar
1 tsp. vanilla
2 tbsps. flour

¼ tsp. salt
½ tsp. baking powder
1½ cups shredded coconut
1 cup chopped, unsalted macadamia
  nuts
1½ cups powdered sugar
2 tbsps. pineapple juice
1 tbsp. lemon juice

Make a pastry base by creaming butter, then adding sugar slowly. Add egg and beat until light and fluffy. Add flour and salt to the butter-sugar mixture and blend well. Pat dough into the bottom of an oblong pan. Bake in a 350° oven for 15 minutes, then cool. Combine the next 8 ingredients and mix well. Pour over the cooled pastry base. Bake in a 350° oven for 20 minutes. Cool. Spread with frosting made of powdered sugar thinned with pineapple and lemon juices. Cut into bars.

— — —

* MAGIC COOKIE BARS *   350° oven

1½ cups corn flakes crumbs
3 tbsps. sugar
½ cup margarine or butter, melted
1 cup chopped nuts

1 (6 oz.) pkg. chocolate chips
1½ cups flaked coconut
1 can Eagle Brand milk

Mix together cornflakes, sugar and melted butter in pan, then pat down to form a crust. Sprinkle walnuts, chocolate chips and coconut over crust. Pour milk over top and bake in a 350° oven for 25 minutes or until brown. Cool, then cut into squares. Makes 1 dozen.

— — —

* ORANGE BLOSSOM SQUARES *   350° oven

2½ cups flour, sifted
2 tsps. baking powder
½ tsp. salt
1½ cups sugar
¾ cup oil

1 tsp. vanilla
½ cup milk
2 eggs
1 (6 oz.) pkg. semi-sweet chocolate
  chips

Sift together flour, baking powder and salt. Set aside. Blend sugar, oil and vanilla. Beat in eggs and stir in flour mixture alternately with the milk. Fold in chocolate. Pour into greased, waxed paper lined, 15x10x1 inch pan. Bake in a 350° oven for 40 to 50 minutes. While hot, spread with the Orange Glaze recipe that follows. Let stand for 24 hours before cutting and serving.
Orange Glaze:
Combine 1 cup powdered sugar, 2 tbsps. orange juice, ½ tsp. shredded
continued

orange rind and stir until smooth. Spread over hot uncut squares. Makes 24, 2½ inch squares.

– – –

CAKES AND PIES

* APPLE CAKE *   350° oven

2½ cups apples
½ cup shortening
1¾ cups sugar
cinnamon, nutmeg
2 tsps. soda

½ cup water
1 cup pecans
1 cup raisins
3 eggs, slightly beaten
3 cups flour

Dice apples. Cream together the shortening, sugar and spices. Add soda which has been dissolved in water. Add apples, nuts, raisins, eggs and then the flour. Bake in a 350° oven for about 45 minutes.

— — —

* GOURMET APPLESAUCE CAKE *   350° oven

1½ cups raisins
¾ cup vegetable shortening
2 cups sugar
3 eggs
2½ cups flour
3 tbsps. cocoa

2 tsps. cinnamon
2 tsps. baking soda
½ tsp. nutmeg
½ tsp. salt
2 cups applesauce
1 cup walnuts

Cover the raisins with boiling water. Let them soak for 30 minutes, then drain. Cream the shortening, gradually adding the sugar and cream until very smooth. Add 1 egg at a time, beating hard after each addition. Sift the flour with the cocoa, cinnamon, baking soda, nutmeg and salt. Stir the dry ingredients into the creamed mixture. Alternate with the applesauce. Add the raisins and the walnuts. When mixed well, pour into an oiled 10 inch tube pan and bake in a 350° oven for 1 hour, or until it tests done with a toothpick. Cool the cake in the pan for about 10 minutes, then remove from pan and finish cooling on a wire rack. To keep this cake for a length of time, wrap in a cloth soaked in wine.

— — —

* PINEAPPLE NUT CAKE *   325° oven

1 small can (8 oz.) crushed
    pineapple
½ cup butter
1 cup sugar
2 eggs, well beaten

¾ cup flour
¼ tsp. baking soda
1 tsp. salt
½ cup chopped nuts
1 cup sweet whipped cream

Drain the pineapple. Melt the butter and pour it into a mixing bowl. Add sugar, beating constantly. Add eggs, flour, soda and salt together and then add to the sugar mixture, stirring until blended. Add the drained pineapple and nuts and mix well. Pour batter into a 9 inch square pan and bake in a 325° oven for 1 hour. Serve with whipped cream.

— — —

* CARROT CAKE *   350° oven

2 cups sugar
2 cups flour
2 tsps. soda
2 tsps. cinnamon
1 tsp. salt

1½ cups oil
4 eggs
3 cups grated carrots
1 cup walnuts

Mix together the first 5 ingredients and then add the rest of the ingredients. Add the eggs 1 at a time. Blend together by hand. Bake in a 350°
oven for 35 minutes. While cake is still warm, spread with Carrot Cake
Icing.

* CARROT CAKE ICING *

1 (8 oz.) pkg. cream cheese
½ stick margarine
1 box powdered sugar

1 tbsp. vanilla
1 cup chopped walnuts

Blend softened cream cheese with the other ingredients. Spread on
warm carrot cake.

— — —

* YUMMY LEMON CAKE *

1 pkg. lemon cake mix

1 pkg. lemon Jello pudding

Prepare according to package directions for 1 layer. While cake is still
hot, pierce with a fork many times. Prepare the pudding by dissolving
it in 1 cup of very hot water. Pour the pudding over the hot cake. Let
this set for several hours before serving. Sprinkle with powdered sugar.

— — —

* STEVE'S FAVORITE CHEESECAKE *   350° oven

2 cups zwieback crumbs, crushed
  fine
1½ cups sugar
1 tsp. cinnamon
½ cup butter, melted
4 eggs
⅛ tsp. salt

1½ tsps. lemon juice
1½ tsps. grated lemon rind
1 cup cream
1½ lbs. cottage cheese
3 tbsps. flour
¼ cup chopped nuts

Mix the zwieback with a ½ cup of sugar, cinnamon and butter. Set aside ¾ of a cup to sprinkle over top, press remainder of crumbs into a 9 inch spring form pan, lining the bottom and sides. Beat eggs until light and foamy, then gradually beat in the remaining cup of sugar. Beat until light. Blend in salt, lemon juice and rind, cream, cottage cheese and flour. Strain through a fine sieve. Pour into lined pan, sprinkle with remaining crumbs and nut meats. Bake in a 350° oven for about 1 hour, or until the center is firm. Turn off heat, open door, let stand in the oven for an hour or until cooled.

— — —

* MANGO UPSIDE-DOWN CAKE *   375° oven

2 cups sliced ripe mangoes
2 tbsps. lemon juice
1 tbsp. margarine
⅓ cup brown sugar, packed
¼ cup oil
¼ tsp. salt

¾ cup sugar
1 egg, well beaten
½ cup milk
1¼ cups flour
2 tsps. baking powder

Sprinkle the lemon juice over the sliced mangoes. Melt the margarine in an 8 inch cake pan. Sprinkle the brown sugar evenly over the margarine. Place the mangoes on top of the brown sugar. In a mixing bowl, cream oil and sugar thoroughly. Add the egg and mix again. Sift dry ingredients and add alternately with the milk. Pour the batter over the mangoes. Bake about 1 hour in a 375° oven. When cake is done, remove from oven and turn it upside-down. Serve warm. Variation: bake in muffin tins for individual servings. Garnish with whipped cream.

— — —

* LEMON PUDDING CAKE *

1 pkg. (18½ oz.) yellow cake mix
1 pkg. (3¾ oz.) lemon pudding
1 tbsp. grated lemon peel

1 pkg. fluffy white frosting mix
½ cup toasted coconut
ice cream

Bake the cake in a jelly roll pan, measuring 15½x10½x1 inches, according to package directions. Prepare the lemon pudding according to package directions. Stir in lemon peel and cool. Prepare frosting mix according to directions. Spread lemon pudding evenly over the cake, then
continued

spread frosting over the pudding. Sprinkle with the shredded, toasted coconut. Serve with ice cream.

— — —

* CHOCOLATE-GLAZED BUTTER RUM CAKE * 350° oven

1 cup butter	2 tsps. baking soda
2 cups sugar	½ tsp. salt
1½ tsps. vanilla	1 cup milk
3 eggs	¾ cup semi-sweet chocolate chips
3 cups unsifted flour	½ cup finely chopped walnuts

Combine butter, sugar and vanilla in a large mixer bowl and cream until light and fluffy. Add eggs, one at a time, beating well. Combine flour, baking soda and salt and add alternately with milk, beating until smooth. Reserve 1½ cups of the batter and pour the remaining batter into a well-greased and floured 10 inch tube pan. Combine chocolate chips and nuts. Sprinkle evenly over the batter in the pan. Spoon reserved batter onto filling, carefully spreading with a spatula to cover. Bake in a 350° oven for 50 to 55 minutes until cake tests done. Cool for 15 minutes in the pan. Carefully pierce the entire surface of the cake with a fork. Gradually spoon half of the Butter Rum Syrup onto cake. Remove cake from pan and invert onto serving plate. Spoon remaining syrup over cake. Allow cake to absorb all the syrup. Cool completely. Glaze the sides of the cake with Chocolate Glaze. Garnish the top of the cake with whipped cream.

* BUTTER RUM SYRUP *

2 tbsps. butter	½ cup sugar
2 tbsps. water	⅓ cup rum

Combine butter, water and sugar in a small saucepan. Boil for 2 minutes, stirring occasionally. Remove from heat and stir in rum.

* CHOCOLATE GLAZE *

½ cup semi-sweet chocolate chips   1½ tsps. butter

Combine ingredients in the top of a double boiler. Stir over hot, not boiling, water until chips are melted and mixture is smooth.

— — —

* CHOCOLATE ICEBOX CAKE *

1 envelope unflavored gelatin	2 eggs, slightly beaten
¼ cup cold water	1 tsp. vanilla
2 tbsps. sugar	2 egg whites, stiffly beaten
dash of salt	1 cup heavy cream
⅓ cup hot water	1½ dozen ladyfingers, split
½ lb. sweet chocolate	

Soak gelatin in cold water. Combine sugar, salt, water and chocolate in the top of a double boiler. Place over simmering water and cook until chocolate is melted. Slowly add egg yolks stirring vigorously until smooth. Cook 2 minutes longer. Add vanilla and gelatin. Cool. Fold in egg whites and chill in the refrigerator until partially set. Then beat up the mixture and fold in whipped cream. Line the bottom and sides of a 1½ quart mold with waxed paper. Arrange split ladyfingers on the bottom and the sides. Pour 1/3 of the chocolate mixture over the ladyfingers. Add another layer of ladyfingers and then more filling. Repeat process until all of the filling is used. Top with ladyfingers. Chill overnight in the refrigerator. Unmold and serve.

— — —

* QUICK ISLAND CAKE *   350° oven

1 pkg. banana cake mix	1 cup orange juice
1 pkg. instant coconut pudding	½ cup salad oil
1 cup eggs	

Combine all of the ingredients in a large bowl and blend at low speed for 8 minutes. Pour into a 10 inch tube pan. Bake in a 350° oven for 50 to 60 minutes. Cool in the pan for 15 minutes and remove to cool on a rack. Frost with Orange Coconut Glaze.

* ORANGE COCONUT GLAZE *

2 tbsps. light cream	1 tbsp. orange juice
1 tbsp. butter, melted	1 tsp. orange rind, grated
2 cups powdered sugar	½ cup coconut flakes

Combine all of the above ingredients except the coconut flakes and beat thoroughly. Stir in the coconut and then pour over the cooled cake. Let the glaze dribble down the sides.

— — —

* SHERRY CAKE *   350° oven

1 pkg. yellow cake mix	¾ cup salad oil
1 pkg. instant vanilla pudding	¾ cup sherry
4 eggs	1 tsp. nutmeg

continued

Put all ingredients in a bowl and beat for 5 minutes at medium speed. Pour it into a greased 10 inch tube or bundt pan. Bake in a 350° oven for 45 minutes or until done. A nice topping for this cake is Orange Sherry Glaze.

* ORANGE SHERRY GLAZE *

1 (16 oz.) jar orange marmalade   3 tbsps. sherry

Mix in saucepan, heat to boiling, stirring occasionally. Reduce heat and simmer for 5 minutes. Cool to room temperature, then drizzle on top of the Sherry Cake.

– – –

* BANANA ICE BOX CAKE *

1 tbsp. unflavored gelatin	6 tbsps. sugar
⅓ cup cold water	2 dozen ladyfingers
1¼ cups mashed ripe bananas	1¼ cups evaporated milk or
¼ tsp. salt	whipping cream
3 tbsps. lemon juice	

If you use the evaporated milk, heat the can in water at simmering temperature for 20 minutes. Chill the milk or whipping cream thoroughly and whip with an egg beater until the mixture is stiff. Soak the gelatin in the cold water for 5 minutes and then melt it by placing over boiling water. Combine gelatin, mashed bananas, salt, lemon juice and sugar. Cool. When the mixture begins to thicken fold in the whipped milk or cream. Line the pan with ladyfingers and cover with part of the banana mixture. Alternate layers of ladyfingers with layers of the banana mixture. Chill thoroughly before serving. Serve with whipped cream.

– – –

* ORANGE CHIP CAKE *   350° oven

½ cup shortening	¼ cup grated orange peel
½ cup granulated sugar	¼ cup chopped walnuts
½ cup brown sugar	2 cups sifted cake flour
1 tsp. vanilla	1 tsp. baking powder
2 eggs, well beaten	1 tsp. baking soda
1 cup semi-sweet chocolate bits,	¼ tsp. salt
chopped fine	1 cup sour milk

Cream shortening, sugars, and vanilla together. Add eggs and beat well. Stir in chocolate, nuts and orange peel. Add sifted dry ingredients alternately with the sour milk. Line a 9 inch square pan with oiled wax paper and pour batter into prepared pan. Bake in a 350° oven for 50 minutes. When cool, frost with Chocolate Wonder Icing. (see next page)

– – –

* CHOCOLATE WONDER ICING *

Melt 3 squares unsweetened chocolate over hot water. Remove from heat, add 1 cup confectioners' sugar and 2 tbsps. hot water. Blend. Add 1 whole beaten egg. Beat in 4 tbsps. butter, 1 tbsp. at a time. Add 1 tsp. of vanilla, mix well and spread over cake.

— — —

* CHOCOLATE MAYONNAISE CAKE *   325° oven

2 cups flour	⅓ cup cocoa
1 tsp. baking powder	¾ cup mayonnaise
½ tsp. baking soda	1 cup water
1¼ cups sugar	1 tsp. vanilla

Mix the above ingredients well, then pour into a greased oblong cake pan and bake in a 350° oven for 35 minutes. Serve with ice cream.

— — —

* RUM CAKE *   325° oven

CAKE:

1 cup chopped pecans	½ cup dark rum
1 (18 oz.) pkg. yellow cake mix	1 (3¾ oz.) pkg. instant vanilla
4 eggs	pudding mix
½ cup salad oil	

GLAZE:

¼ lb. butter	1 cup sugar
¼ cup water	½ cup dark rum

Grease and flour a 12 cup bundt or tube pan. Sprinkle nuts over the bottom of the pan. Mix all cake ingredients together and pour over the nuts. Bake in 325° oven for 1 hour. When done, invert onto a serving plate. Prick the top with a fork. Drizzle and smooth a portion of the glaze evenly over the top of the cake. Allow cake to absorb the glaze and then repeat. Use all the glaze.
GLAZE: Melt the butter in a saucepan. Stir in the water and sugar. Boil for 5 minutes, stirring constantly. Remove from heat and stir in rum.

— — —

* LEMON JELLO CAKE *   350° oven

1 pkg. yellow cake mix	¾ cup cold water
1 pkg. lemon Jello	¾ cup vegetable oil
4 large eggs	

Mix all ingredients and beat well. Pour into an oblong baking pan which has been greased and floured. Bake in a 350° oven for 35 to 40 minutes. While still hot, pierce cake many times with a fork and then cover with the following glaze.
GLAZE: Mix together 2 cups powdered sugar and the juice of 2 lemons. Pour over the hot cake.

— — —

* CHOCOLATE ALMOND SPONGE CAKE *   350° oven

2 eggs, separated	1 cup cake flour
½ cup water	2 tbsps. cocoa
1 cup sugar	¾ tsp. baking powder
½ tsp. almond extract	¼ tsp. salt

Grease and flour two 8 inch pans. Beat egg yolks with water until very thick, about 10 minutes. Add extract. Beat egg whites until stiff, then fold into a batter of the rest of the ingredients combined. Pour into pans and bake in a 350° oven for 25 to 30 minutes. When cool, frost with Chocolate Almond Frosting.

* CHOCOLATE ALMOND FROSTING *

¾ cup butter or margarine, softened	⅓ cup cocoa
1 cup sifted powdered sugar	1 tsp. almond extract

Combine ingredients and beat until smooth.

— — —

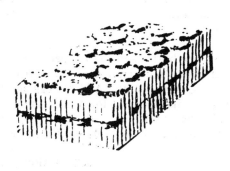

* MAYONNAISE DATE CAKE *   325° oven

¾ cup chopped dates	1½ tsp. cinnamon
2¼ cups water	¾ tsp. ground cloves
1½ cups mayonnaise	3 tsps. baking soda
1½ cups sugar	1½ tsps. vanilla
3 cups flour	1½ cups chopped walnuts

Boil dates for 5 minutes in the water and let cool. Cream the mayonnaise and sugar. Sift together the flour, cinnamon, ground cloves and baking soda. Add vanilla and nuts. Add the dates and the water that they were boiled in. Mix well and pour into a greased oblong baking pan and bake in a 325° oven for 30 to 40 minutes. Serve topped with whipped cream.

— — —

* CATHY'S FESTIVE CHOCOLATE ICEBOX CAKE *
(for the devoted chocolate fan)

½ lb. sweet chocolate	3 tbsps. water
1 square bitter or semi-sweet chocolate	4 eggs, separated
	18 ladyfingers, split
3 tbsps. sugar	½ pint whipping cream

Melt the chocolate in the top of a double boiler, then add sugar, water and well beaten egg yolks. Cook slowly until thick and smooth, stirring constantly. Remove from heat and let cool, then fold in stiffly beaten egg whites. Pour this mixture into a 7 inch spring form pan lined on the bottom and sides with split ladyfingers. Chill thoroughly. When ready to serve, whip the cream and spread on top of cake. Add a few shavings of chocolate for decoration. Serve only small pieces as this is very rich.

— — —

* COCONUT UPSIDE-DOWN CAKE *   350° oven

½ cup butter or margarine	1¼ cups sifted flour
1 cup brown sugar	2 tsps. baking powder
1½ cup coconut	¼ tsp. salt
¼ cup shortening	½ cup milk
¾ cup sugar	½ tsp. vanilla
1 egg	

Melt the butter and sugar together in the bottom of an 8x8x2 inch pan. Sprinkle the coconut over the bottom. Cream the shortening and add the sugar gradually. Add the egg and beat well. Sift together the dry ingredients and add them alternately with milk to the sugar mixture. Add the vanilla. Pour the batter over the coconut mixture. Bake in a 350° oven until done, about 40 minutes.

— — —

* PINEAPPLE CAKE *   350° oven

3 tbsps. butter or margarine	10 to 12 maraschino cherries
½ cup brown sugar	yellow or white cake mix, prepared
6 slices canned pineapple, well drained	

Melt the butter in a square pan. Add the brown sugar and pineapple slices and cherries. Fill 2/3 full with cake batter and bake in a 350° oven for 40 minutes.

— — —

* GUAVA ICE BOX CAKE *

2 tsps. gelatin	⅓ cup shredded pineapple
3 tbsps. cold water	2 tbsps. lemon juice
⅔ cup sugar	2 beaten egg whites
3 tbsps. boiling water	8 ladyfingers

continued

⅔ cup fresh or cooked guava pulp ½ cup whipping cream
   (pressed through a sieve before
   measuring)

Soak gelatin in cold water for a few minutes; add it and the sugar to the boiling water and stir until dissolved. Cool. Add the fruit pulp and the juice to the gelatin and mix thoroughly. Place in the refrigerator to congeal. When the mixture is partially hardened, beat until foamy. Then fold in the beaten egg whites. Line a spring-form pan with the ladyfingers halves, pour in the gelatin mixture and then chill at least 4 to 6 hours. Turn out on a serving platter and garnish with whipped cream just before serving. A dab of guava jelly will decorate the whipped cream.

— — —

* CHEESE CAKE *   300 ° oven

1 lb. cream cheese broken up with ¼ cup flour
   a fork   ½ pint sour cream
yolk of 4 eggs   1 tsp. vanilla or lemon juice and rind
1 scant cup of sugar

Beat the above together and fold into 4 well beaten egg whites. Bake in a spring-form pan lined with melba toast, zwieback, vanilla wafers or graham crackers, all crushed. (Crust may be omitted.) Bake in a 350 ° oven for about 1 hour. When done, turn oven off, open oven door, and leave cake inside to cool off gradually with the oven. This will help to prevent the cake from dropping. Serve when cool.

— — —

* MOCHA PECAN CAKE *   325 ° oven

1 tbsp. instant coffee   4 cups sifted flour
3 tbsps. hot water   1 tsp. baking powder
2 cups butter, softened   ¼ tsp. salt
1 cup sugar   ½ cup milk
1½ cups brown sugar   ¾ tsp. rum extract
6 eggs   3 cups chopped pecans

Dissolve the coffee in the hot water. Cream together the softened butter and the sugars. Beat in the eggs, 1 at a time. Sift flour with baking powder and salt. Add alternately with the milk, coffee and rum extract. Fold in the chopped nuts. Pour batter into a greased tube or bundt pan. Bake in a 325 ° oven for 1½ hours. The following icing is optional. ICING: Mix together 1 cup of whipping cream, 3 to 4 tbsps. brown sugar and ½ to 1 tsp. instant coffee. Spread over the top of the warm cake.

— — —

* HAWAIIAN FRUIT CAKE *   300° oven

2 cups flour, sifted
1 tsp. baking powder
½ tsp. salt
1 cup grated coconut
6 to 8 slices of candied pineapple,
  cut into narrow wedges
½ lb. maraschino cherries, or red
  candied cherries, whole

1½ cups chopped macadamia nuts,
  unsalted
½ cup citron, chopped
½ cup orange and lemon peel
1 cup butter
1 cup sugar
3 eggs, beaten
½ cup sherry

Line cake pans or 1 lb. coffee cans with heavy paper that has been buttered. Heavy waxed freezer paper will also work. Sift together the flour, baking powder and salt. Resift into a bowl containing the fruit and the nuts. Cream the butter, gradually adding the sugar, then the eggs and blend thoroughly. Fold into flour mixture. Mix well, then add the sherry. Stir until completely blended. Fill the lined cake pans ¾ full with cake batter and bake on the center rack of the oven over a pan containing 1 inch of hot water. Bake in a 300° oven for 1½ hours. Remove pan of water. At this time, it is possible to decorate the cakes.
Combine:

½ cup candied pineapple wedges
¾ cup candied cherries
⅓ cup citron

¾ cup chopped macadamia nuts,
  unsalted

Decorate the tops of the cakes when they come out of the oven. The fruit syrup will moisten the nuts so that they will glaze during the rest of the baking. Bake cakes for ½ hour more, for a total cooking time of 2 hours. Cool cakes in the pans. Remove and wrap cakes in fresh wax paper and then foil.

— — —

* AVOCADO CHIFFON PIE *

baked 9 inch pie shell
1 tbsp. gelatin
¼ cup cold water
1 cup strained avocado pulp
3 eggs, separated
1 cup sugar

¼ tsp. salt
½ tsp. nutmeg
1 tsp. cinnamon
1½ tbsps. butter
2 tbsps. lemon juice

Mix gelatin in cold water. Wait for 5 minutes before using. Meanwhile, mix together avocado, egg yolks, ½ cup sugar, salt, nutmeg and cinnamon. Cook over low heat, stirring constantly until slightly thickened. Remove from heat and add butter, lemon juice and softened gelatin. Mix well and let cool. Beat egg whites until stiff but not dry. Gradually add ½ cup sugar and beat thoroughly. Fold gelatin mixture into egg whites. Pour into shell and chill until firm. Sprinkle nutmeg for garnish.

— — —

* HAUPIA PUMPKIN PIE *   425° oven

1 can (1 lb.) pumpkin
2 eggs, slightly beaten
¾ cup sugar
½ tsp. salt
1 tsp. cinnamon
½ tsp. ginger
¼ tsp. cloves

1 can (13 oz.) evaporated skim milk
1½ cups freshly grated coconut
pastry for 9 inch pie shell
1 pkg. haupia pudding mix (2½ oz.)
1 cup whipped cream
1 tbsp. sugar

Combine pumpkin and eggs. Stir in sugar, salt and spices. Add milk and 1 cup grated coconut. Pour into pie shell. Bake for 15 minutes in a 425° oven, then lower heat to 350° and bake 40 to 45 minutes or until filling is set. Cool. Prepare pudding mix according to package directions. Cool slightly, then pour over pie. Chill until haupia is firm. Just before serving, whip cream in a small bowl, add the sugar. Spread over pie. Sprinkle with the remaining coconut.

— — —

* PECAN PIE *   350° oven

½ cup sugar
1 tbsp. flour
⅓ cup butter or margarine
2 eggs

1 tsp. vanilla
1 cup light karo syrup
1 cup pecan meats, broken

Mix sugar and flour. Add butter and work until creamy. Add eggs and beat until smooth. Add vanilla and syrup. Stir in pecans and pour into pastry shell which has been placed in a hot oven until lightly browned. Bake in a 350° oven until center is firm to the touch.

— — —

* PARADISE BANANA PIE *   400° oven

4 cups firm bananas, sliced
¼ cup pineapple juice
2 tbsps. lemon juice
1½ tsps. grated lemon rind

¼ cup sugar
½ tsp. cinnamon
1 tsp. cornstarch
pastry for 8 inch pie crust

Soak bananas in pineapple and lemon juice for 20 minutes. Drain and save juices. Sprinkle grated lemon rind, sugar and cinnamon over banana slices. Toss lightly and place in a pie plate lined in pastry. Warm juices saved from before and thicken with cornstarch. Add this mixture to the pie. Cover with the following topping.

Topping:
⅓ cup chopped macadamia nuts
¾ cup flour
¾ cup brown sugar

¾ tsp. cinnamon
6 tbsps. butter

Combine all of the ingredients and cut with a pastry blender or 2 knives until lumpy, loose mixture forms. Sprinkle over bananas. Bake in a 400° oven for 20 minutes or until crust is brown.

— — —

* GLAZED STRAWBERRY PIE *

9 inch baked pastry shell or
  graham cracker crust
4 cups ripe strawberries
⅔ cup sugar

1 tsp. lemon juice
1 cup water
3 tbsps. cornstarch

Arrange 2 cups of the choicest strawberries in the baked pie shell. Crush the remaining berries. Add the sugar, lemon juice and water in a saucepan and bring to a boil. Blend cornstarch with a little cold water and stir into berry mixture. Cook until mixture is thick and glossy. Cool and pour over berries. Refrigerate until serving time. Any local berry such as the thimbleberry can be adapted to this recipe.

— — —

* BANANA CREAM PIE *   300° - 325° oven

1½ cups milk
3 tbsps. cornstarch
½ cup sugar
1 tbsp. butter
¼ tsp. salt
½ tsp. vanilla

1 cup sliced bananas
2 egg yolks
2 tbsps. sugar
2 egg whites
baked 8 inch pie shell

Mix cornstarch, sugar and salt, add 3 tbsps. of the milk and mix to a smooth paste. Heat remaining milk and slowly pour in the cornstarch mixture, stirring constantly. Cook over hot water for 20 minutes, cool slightly and add egg yolks to the mixture slowly, stirring rapidly. Cook several minutes until it thickens. Remove from heat, cool and add vanilla. Arrange slices of banana in the pie shell, pour in custard mixture and cover top with meringue, made of stiffly beaten egg whites and the sugar. Brown in a slow oven, 300° to 325° for about 20 minutes.

— — —

* COCONUT MERINGUE PIE *   325° oven

⅔ cup sugar
½ cup flour
⅛ tsp. salt
2 cups milk
3 eggs, separated

1 tsp. vanilla
½ cup grated coconut
4 to 6 tbsps. sugar
1 baked pie shell

Mix the dry ingredients. Add the milk gradually. Cook mixture for 15 minutes in a double boiler, stirring constantly until it thickens. Add some of the hot mixture to the slightly beaten egg whites. Add this to the milk mixture and cook for 3 minutes longer. Cool and add the vanilla and the coconut. Pour mixture into the baked pie shell and cover, while still hot, with meringue made by beating the egg whites stiff and adding the sugar gradually, beating well after each addition. Be sure that the meringue touches the pastry around the whole pie. Sprinkle with some more coconut and bake in a 325° oven until top is light brown.

— — —

* COCONUT CREAM PIE *

½ cup sugar
3 tbsps. cornstarch
pinch of salt
2 cups milk
3 egg yolks

½ tsp. vanilla
½ cup whipping cream
¾ cup fresh grated coconut
baked pie shell

Combine the sugar, cornstarch and salt. Scald the milk and add the dry ingredients slowly to the hot milk, stirring until a smooth mixture is obtained. Cook over hot water, stirring frequently. Cool the mixture to lukewarm and stir in the egg yolks. Cook over hot water until the custard thickens. Cool, add vanilla, pour into a baked pie shell. Chill and whip the cream. Just before serving, spread the whipped cream over the custard and sprinkle with coconut.

— — —

* COCONUT CHIFFON PIE *

1 large pkg. coconut cream pudding
1½ cups milk
1 tsp. almond extract

½ cup flaked coconut
1 large carton Cool Whip, cooled
1 large pastry shell, 9 inch

Prepare pastry crust. After rolling out to size, sprinkle with ¼ cup of coconut and roll again to press in the coconut. Fit pastry into a pan, bake and cool. Prepare pudding mix according to directions on package, except use only 1½ cups of milk. Add almond extract and cool. Blend Cool Whip into pudding mix. Pour into cooked shell. Toast ¼ cup of flaked coconut in oven until a little brown. Sprinkle on top of pie. Chill 2 hours.

— — —

* MACADAMIA NUT PIE I *

1 large pkg. instant vanilla pudding
1½ cups milk
1 tsp. vanilla extract
1 large carton Cool Whip, thawed

⅔ cup ground, unsalted macadamia
nuts
9 inch pastry shell

Prepare pastry crust. After rolling to size, sprinkle with some of the ground nuts and roll again to press nuts into crust. Fit into pie pan, bake and cool. Prepare instant pudding according to directions, except use only 1½ cups of cool milk. Add vanilla extract and the rest of the ground nuts. Reserve some for garnish if desired. Fold pudding into thawed Cool Whip. Pour into cooled pastry shell. Sprinkle with the reserved nuts on top. Chill for 2 hours.

— — —

* MACADAMIA NUT PIE II *   350° oven

¼ lb. butter
¾ cup sugar
3 eggs, slightly beaten
¾ cup dark corn syrup
¼ tsp. salt

1 tsp. vanilla
1 cup chopped, unsalted
  macadamia nuts
1 unbaked pie shell

Cream the butter, add the sugar gradually. When light and lemon colored, add the beaten eggs. Blend in dark corn syrup. Add the salt, vanilla and nuts. Mix well, then pour into the unbaked pie shell. Bake in a 350° oven for 35 to 40 minutes.

— — —

* GRASSHOPPER PIE *   350° oven

20 plain chocolate wafers   ⅓ cup melted butter

Roll cookies into fine crumbs. Mix with the butter and press into a lightly buttered 9 inch pie pan. Bake in a 350° oven for 10 minutes. Cool.

25 large marshmallows
½ cup milk
2 oz. creme de menthe
1 oz. white creme de menthe

½ pint whipping cream
½ cup whipping cream
shaved or grated semi-sweet
  chocolate

Melt the marshmallows in the milk over hot water. Cool, add the liqueurs and beat thoroughly. Fold in the cream, whipped to soft peaks. Pour into the crust, holding out ½ cup. Refrigerate until partially set. Pour remaining ½ cup of cream in the center of the pie. Refrigerate for several hours. Whip the remaining cream, and spread over the top. Cover with the shaved or grated chocolate.

— — —

* PERFECT PEACH PIE *

2 (29 oz.) cans peach slices
½ cup sugar
1 envelope unflavored gelatin
⅓ cup orange juice
3 tbsps. brandy
2 tbsps. lemon juice

1 tbsp. butter
1 cup fresh or frozen blueberries,
  thawed
baked 9 inch pie shell
6 pastry strips, ¾ inch wide and 4
  inches long, baked

Drain the peaches well, reserving 1¼ cups syrup. Reserve a few peach slices for garnish. In a saucepan, combine sugar, gelatin, and the reserved peach syrup. Heat and stir until gelatin is dissolved, about 3 minutes. Stir in orange juice, brandy, lemon juice, and butter. Fold in peaches, then blueberries. Turn mixture into pastry shell, then top with pastry strips in a spoke fashion. Chill until firm. Garnish with reserved peaches.

— — —

* PAPAYA PIE *   425 ° oven

1 cup pineapple juice
¾ cup sugar
3 cups chopped, firm papaya
⅓ cup cornstarch

⅓ cup water
1 tbsp. butter or margarine
pastry for 2 crust pie

Combine juice and sugar, and bring to a boil. Add papaya. Cook until the papaya is tender. Strain fruit carefully and set aside. Combine cornstarch and water, stir into juice. Cook until mixture thickens, stirring constantly. Return papaya to liquid, then add butter and cool. Pour filling into pastry shell. Cut remaining dough in ½ inch strips, about 11 inches long. Weave a lattice work on waxed paper and invert onto pie. Trim the edge of the pie, seal with water and crimp with a fork. Bake in a 425 ° oven for 25 minutes.

— — —

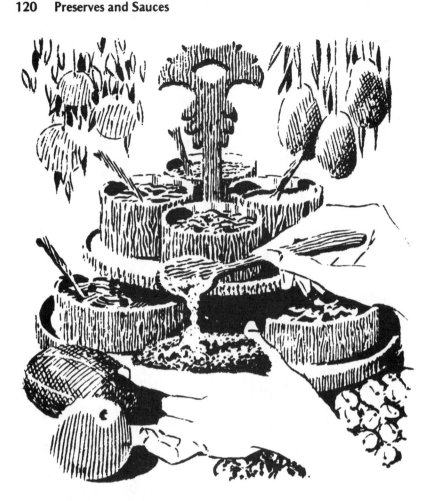

PRESERVES AND SAUCES

* APPLESAUCE *

5 lbs. cored, peeled, sliced apples
3 cups sugar
2 tsps. cinnamon
dashes of nutmeg

½ tsp. ground cloves
juice of 1 lemon
1 quart apple cidar

Mix all of the above and simmer until thick, stirring occasionally. Cool, and add ½ tsp. of vanilla. This is a chunky applesauce, not smooth like the store bought kind. Use as a pie filling also.

— — —

* PINEAPPLE CHUTNEY *

3 lbs. peeled pineapple, chopped   2 tbsps. finely chopped ginger root
1½ pints vinegar   1½ lbs. brown sugar
1 tbsp. salt   ½ lb. seedless raisins
2 oz. small red peppers, chopped   ½ lb. almonds, blanched and
   fine   chopped fine
1 medium sized bulb of garlic, chopped

Cut the pineapple in small pieces, add vinegar and salt, cook slowly until the pineapple is tender. Add the other ingredients and boil slowly
until thick. Pour into hot sterile jars and seal immediately.

— — —

* PINEAPPLE HONEY JAM *

10 cups pineapple, chopped   ½ cup finely chopped ginger root
2 cups orange peel, sliced fine   3 cups honey
2 cups orange sections

Remove rind from 6 oranges, cutting so that the membrane is removed
from the orange pulp. Soak rind in water for ½ hour. Drain and cook
until tender, changing the water 3 times during the cooking time. Drain,
wash with cold water and then remove pulp from the inside of the rind
by scraping with a spoon. Cut rind in narrow strips Remove membrane
from orange sections. Combine pineapple, rind, ginger and honey. Cook
over low heat until pineapple is almost tender. Drain off honey and
evaporate to a thicker consistency over low heat. Pour pineapple into
jars and then fill with honey syrup. Seal immediately.

— — —

* MANGO JAM *

12 cups ripe mango slices   6 cups sugar
4 cups water

Add water to mango slices and cook about 15 minutes or until tender.
Press mangoes through a sieve, add sugar and boil until thick. Pour into
hot sterilized jars and seal with paraffin.

— — —

* PAPAYA CATSUP *

14 cups strained papaya pulp
4 tbsps. whole allspice
3 tbsps. whole cloves
3 tbsps. mustard seed
1 stick cinnamon
1 medium sized piece of ginger
   root, chopped

1 large onion, sliced
1/8 tsp. red pepper
6 tbsps. sugar
2 tbsps. salt
1 1/3 cups vinegar
1/4 tsp. tartaric acid

Tie the spices and onion in a cheesecloth bag, add to the papaya pulp and cook slowly for 40 minutes. Add the sugar, salt, vinegar and tartaric acid. Cook for 1 hour or until thick. Remove spices and pour into hot sterile jars. Seal with paraffin.

— — —

* HAM RAISIN SAUCE *

1 cup sugar
1/2 cup water
1 cup seedless raisins
2 tbsps. butter
3 tbsps. vinegar
1 (6 oz.) jar fruit jelly

1/2 tbsp. Worcestershire sauce
1/2 tsp. salt
1/8 tsp. pepper
1/4 tsp. cloves
few grains of mace

Cook sugar and water for 5 minutes. Add remaining ingredients and cook until jelly dissolves. Serve hot over ham.

— — —

* PICANTI SAUCE *

5 cups canned tomatoes
1 cup onions, put through a
   blender

2 small cans peeled green chilies
1 tsp. salt

Mix ingredients together in a large kettle. Simmer for 15 minutes. Pour into jars and boil in a water bath for 20 minutes. Tighten the rings and seal. Store in a dark place.

— — —

* CRANBERRY RELISH *

1 lb. cranberries
2 large firm tart apples

2 oranges
2 cups sugar

Remove seeds from apples and oranges, but do not skin. Grind the fruit, using a medium blade, then mix with the sugar. This keeps up to about
continued

6 weeks in the refrigerator. It freezes well. Good with ham, poultry and game.

— — —

* PINEAPPLE PICKLE *

3 cups white vinegar
3½ cups sugar
3 cups water

2 tbsps. whole cloves
2 sticks cinnamon
12 cups pineapple pieces

Combine vinegar, sugar and water. Tie spices in cheesecloth and add to mixture. Boil slowly for about 20 minutes. Add pineapple and boil gently in a covered container for 1½ hours, or until tender. Pour into hot sterile jars and seal immediately.

— — —

* PAPAYA PICKLE *

4 cups sugar
2 cups vinegar
12 cloves
16 peppercorns

4 bay leaves
8 cups half-ripe papaya chunks
2 cups water

Make a syrup of sugar and vinegar, cook 6 minutes. Add cloves, peppercorns and bay leaves. Cook papaya slices in the water for 5 minutes and add the drained fruit to the syrup. Cook mixture for 15 minutes, pour into hot sterile jars and seal immediately.

— — —

* POHA SYRUP *

4 cups husked pohas

1 cup sugar for each cup cooked
    fruit

Cook pohas in a little water until soft. Strain through a wire strainer to remove skins. The seeds will sink to the bottom. Pour off the juice, measure, and add an equal amount of sugar. Cook until mixture forms a very soft jelly when cooled. Use on hot cakes, waffles, ice cream or French toast.

— — —

* PINEAPPLE JAM *

12 cups grated or chopped fresh
    pineapple
6 cups sugar

6 tbsps. lemon juice
rind of 3 lemons, sliced in very thin
    slices, ½ inch long

Combine pineapple and sugar and allow to stand overnight. Add lemon juice and rind, then cook slowly for 2 hours. Pour into hot sterile jars and seal with paraffin.

— — —

* PAPAYA JAM *

6 cups ripe papaya pulp   6 cups sugar
1 cup lemon juice

Press papaya through a coarse sieve before measuring. Add lemon and sugar. Boil vigorously for 20 minutes or until thick enough for jam. Stir frequently to prevent scorching. Pour into sterile jars and seal with paraffin.

— — —

* TENNESSEE STRAWBERRY PRESERVES *

2 lbs. hulled and washed   2 lbs. granulated sugar
  strawberries

Put a layer of berries in a kettle, then a layer of sugar, and alternate until all ingredients are used. Cook very slowly over low heat until juice comes out. Stir gently to prevent burning. Boil very gently for 15 minutes. Allow to stand until cold (syrup should be thick) and then pour into sterile jars and seal with paraffin.

— — —

* EAST INDIAN CURRIED PICKLES *

6 large cucumbers, washed, pared   1 small hot red pepper
  and sliced   1 tbsp. curry powder
6 medium onions, washed, peeled   1 tsp. celery seed
  and sliced   1 tsp. mustard seed
1 quart white vinegar   ½ tsp. fresh ground pepper
1½ cups brown sugar   2 tbsps. mixed pickling spice in a bag
salt

Combine cucumbers and onions in a large bowl. Sprinkle ½ cup of salt over vegetables. Add water to cover. Let stand in a cool place overnight. Drain and wash under cold running water. Drain. Spoon into sterile glass jars. Combine the remaining ingredients in an enamel kettle. Cover and boil gently for 10 minutes. Remove spice bag. Pour hot sauce over the vegetables in the jars. Seal at once. Let stand several weeks in a dark cool place.

— — —

* MANGO PICKLE *

9 cups green mango slices   ½ tbsp. whole cloves
6 cups salt water (1 tbsp. salt to   ½ tbsp. whole peppercorns
  1 cup of water)   4 bay leaves
9 cups sugar   4½ cups water
4½ cups vinegar

Soak mango slices overnight in enough salt water to cover. Drain, add
continued

the fresh water and cook until partially tender, about 30 minutes. Add spices and vinegar. Cook about 15 minutes longer, or until mango slices are tender. Drain mangoes and cook syrup until it is slightly thick. Add mangoes, heat to boiling point, and pour into sterile jars. Seal at once.

— — —

* STUFFED DILLS *

Remove the center of a large dill pickle, lengthwise, using an apple corer. Stuff cavity with pimento cream cheese, deviled ham, or cream cheese and anchovy mix. Chill and cut in ½ inch slices. Serve with a toothpick.

— — —

* KOSHER DILL PICKLES *

50 medium cucumbers, approx. 3½ inches long)
FOR EACH JAR:
2 or 3 bay leaves
¼ tsp. celery or mustard seeds
½ tsp. whole mixed spice
1 tbsp. vinegar

3 quarts pickling solution (3 qts. water to ¾ cup salt)

2 cloves garlic
bunch of dry dill
2 grape leaves
⅛ tsp. alum

Wash and drain cucumbers and pack into quart jars. To each jar, add bay leaves, mustard or celery seeds, mixed whole spice, vinegar, garlic and alum in quantities listed. Bring pickling solution to a boil and fill packed jars. Top each jar with a small bunch of dried dill and grape leaves. Adjust covers and seal at once. Can be used after 8 or 10 days. Hints: Don't let the bubbling of the pickles scare you into throwing them away. It's only fermentation. It should stop in 3 to 5 days, after which you should clamp down the cover of the jar. Use coarse salt. It makes a less scummy brine. Dissolve salt in boiling water and let cool before using. Use a high grade of pickling vinegar.

— — —

* MANGO CHUTNEY I *

2 cups vinegar
5½ cups sugar
10 cups green mango slices
1 tsp. salt
½ cup chopped green ginger root
1 clove garlic, chopped fine

4 red peppers, remove seeds
3 cups seedless raisins
1 large onion, sliced
¼ cup fresh orange peel
⅔ cup blanched chopped almonds

Boil vinegar and sugar about 5 minutes. Add sliced mangoes and other ingredients. Mix all ingredients and boil slowly, stirring frequently until thick, about 1½ hour. Place in sterilized jars and seal tightly.

— — —

* MANGO CHUTNEY II *

3½ to 4 cups vinegar
6 cups sugar
12 cups mango slices
½ cup chopped green ginger root
4 chili peppers, chopped fine

1 clove garlic
3 cups raisins
1 large onion, sliced
1 tsp. salt

Boil vinegar and sugar for 5 minutes. Add mango and other ingredients, and cook about 1 hour until thick and of the desired consistency. Pour into sterile glasses and seal immediately.

— — —

* LEMON COCKTAIL SAUCE *

⅓ cup mayonnnaise
1 tsp. horseradish
1 tsp. minced chives

1 tsp. prepared mustard
1 to 2 tbsps. lemon juice

Combine all ingredients and mix well.

— — —

* TOMATO COCKTAIL SAUCE *

½ cup tomato catsup
1 tbsp. lemon juice
1 tbsp. Worcestershire sauce
1 tbsp. horseradish

½ tsp. Tabasco sauce
¼ tsp. salt
1 tsp. minced onion

Mix all of the above ingredients and chill thoroughly.

— — —

* ITALIAN TOMATO SAUCE *

1 tbsp. minced onions
1 tbsp. butter

1 (8 oz.) can tomato sauce
2 tbsps. Parmesan cheese

Saute onions in butter and then add tomato sauce and cheese. Heat through and serve.

— — —

* DILL SAUCE *

Combine ½ cup mayonnaise and 1 tbsp. dried dill.

— — —

* TARTAR SAUCE *

1 cup mayonnaise
1 tbsp. pickle relish
1 tbsp. parsley

1 tbsp. capers
1 tbsp. onion
1 tbsp. green olives

Mix all ingredients and chill thoroughly.

— — —

* CUCUMBER SAUCE *

¼ cup mayonnaise or sour cream   ¼ tsp. chopped onion
½ cup finely diced cucumber   ¼ tsp. celery seeds or chopped celery

Mix all of the above and chill.

— — —

* HOLLANDAISE SAUCE *

2 egg yolks   salt and cayenne pepper to taste
2 tbsps. lemon juice   ¼ lb. butter, melted

Place all items but butter in a blender. Cover, and blend on low speed
for 5 seconds. Remove blender cap. Pour in melted butter in a slow,
steady stream. Continue blending only until sauce has thickened. If the
sauce curdles, add 2 egg yolks and blend at high speed while adding
whipping cream, a tsp. at a time, until it reconstitutes.

— — —

LIST OF CONTRIBUTORS

Betty Anderson
Judy Beeman
Martin Beeman
Peggy Beeman
Roland Ching
Evelyn Crabb
Verna Ferreira
Marcy Frenz
Jane Guthrie
Ernest Halycon
Dorothy Hanks
Fran Hargrove
Charlene Harrington
Mynam Hope
Wendy Hughes
Greta Jaeckle
Ellen Kai

Patricia Macayan
Fern Miller
Alice Nagas
Mrs. W.R. Payne
Evarilla Pontius
Christine Reed
Frances Reed
Stephen Reed
Sally Rota
Cece Ryan
Grace Scowen
Mary Smith
Betty Steuermann
Daniel Thompson
Vivian Thompson
Betty Lou Van Sickle
Norman Vladyka

TABLE OF EQUIVALENTS

almonds. . .1 pound (in the shell)	=	1 cup nut meats
almonds. . .½ pound (shelled)	=	2 cups
arrowroot. . .1½ tsps.	=	1 tbsp. flour
avocado. . . 1 medium	=	2 cups, chopped
baking powder . . .1 tsp.	=	1 tsp. baking soda plus ½ tsp. cream of tartar
bananas. . . 1 pound (4 small)	=	2 cups, mashed
berries. . .1 pint	=	2 cups
butter. . .1 cube	=	½ cup or 8 tbsps.
cabbage. . .1 pound	=	4 cups, shredded
carrots. . .1 pound (8 small)	=	4 cups, chopped
celery. . .1 stalk	=	½ cup, finely chopped
cheese. . .¼ pound (grated)	=	1 cup
chocolate. . .1 ounce (1 square)	=	4 tbsps., grated
chocolate. . .1 ounce (1 square)	=	3 tbsps. cocoa plus 1 tbsp. shortening
coconut. . .½ pound	=	2½ cups, shredded
coffee. . .1 pound (80 tbsps.)	=	40 to 50 cups coffee
coffee. . .4 ounces (instant)	=	60 cups coffee
cornstarch. . .1½ tsp.	=	1 tbsp. flour
cottage cheese. . .½ pound	=	1 cup
crab. . .½ pound (fresh or frozen; cooked or canned)	=	1 cup meat
cream cheese. . .3 ounces	=	6 tbsps.
cream. . .1 cup (heavy whipping)	=	2 cups, whipped

continued

TABLE OF EQUIVALENTS continued

eggs. . .6 medium (raw, whole)	=	1 cup
egg whites. . .1 medium	=	1½ tbsps.
egg whites. . .9 medium	=	1 cup
egg yolks. . .1 medium	=	1 tbsp.
egg yolks. . .16 medium	=	1 cup
escargots. . .6 snails	=	1½ ounces
flour. . .1 pound (all purpose)	=	4 cups, sifted
flour. . .1 pound (cake, sifted)	=	4½ cups
garlic powder. . .& tsp.	=	1 small clove garlic
gelatin. . .¼ oz. envelope (powdered)	=	1 scant tbsp.
ginger. . .½ tsp. (powdered)	=	1 tsp., fresh
herbs. . .½ tsp. (dried)	=	1 tbsp., fresh
ice cubes. . .2 cubes	=	¼ cup
lemon. . .1 medium	=	3 tbsps. juice and 2 tsps. grated peel
lobster. . .½ pound (cooked)	=	1 cup meat
mushrooms. . .½ pound (fresh, 20 medium)	=	2 cups, raw, sliced
mushrooms. . .3 ounces (dried)	=	1 pound fresh
onions. . .1 medium	=	1 cup, finely chopped
orange. . .1 small	=	6 tbsps. juice and 1 tbsp. grated peel
oysters. . .½ pound (raw)	=	1 cup
papaya. . .1 medium	=	1½ cups, chopped
peanuts. . .1 pound (in the shell)	=	2 cups nut meats
peanuts. . .½ pound (shelled)	=	1 cup
pecans. . .1 pound (in the shell)	=	2½ cups nut meats
pecans. . .½ pound (shelled)	=	2 cups
pineapple. . .1 medium	=	2½ cups, chopped
potatoes. . .1 pound (4 medium)	=	2½ cups, cooked and diced
rice. . .1 pound (2½ cups)	=	8 cups, cooked
scallops. . .½ pound (shucked)	=	1 cup
shrimp. . .1 pound (cooked)	=	3 cups
spinach. . .1 pound (fresh)	=	2 cups
tea leaves. . .1 pound	=	300 cups tea
tomatoes. . .1 pound (3 medium)	=	1¼ cups, cooked, chopped
tuna. . .6½ oz. (canned, drained)	=	¾ cup
walnuts. . .1 pound (in the shell)	=	2½ cups nut meats
walnuts. . .½ pound (shelled)	=	2 cups

INDEX

continued

POULTRY   pg.

MEAT AND CASSEROLE   pg.

VEGETABLES   pg.

continued

132   Index

BREADS AND PASTRIES   pg.

DESSERTS AND GOODIES   pg.

continued

My Recipes

My Recipes

My Recipes